Unity in truth

Unity in truth

Addresses given by Dr D. Martyn Lloyd-Jones
at meetings held under the auspices of the
British Evangelical Council

edited by Hywel R. Jones

 EVANGELICAL PRESS

EVANGELICAL PRESS
12 Wooler Streer, Darlington, Co. Durham, DL1 1RQ, England

British Library Cataloguing in Publication Data available.

ISBN 0 85234 288 8

Scripture quotations are from the Authorized (King James) Version.

Printed and bound in Great Britain at the Bath Press, Bath, Avon.

Contents

1.
The Doctor and the British Evangelical Council

The late Doctor D. Martyn Lloyd-Jones was as concerned for the unity of churches which were committed to the Christian gospel as he was for the maintenance of the gospel itself. The addresses which he gave under the auspices of the British Evangelical Council are proof positive of that. They are reproduced in this volume. Two collections of other addresses which he gave have recently been published. These are entitled *The Puritans* and *Knowing the Times*. In the introduction to the latter, reference was made to this projected publication, which should be read in association with those books as well as, of course, the second volume of the Doctor's authorized biography. Speaking very broadly, the Doctor was concerned with major lessons from the past in *The Puritans* and with the signifi-cance of events in the mid-twentieth century in *Knowing the Times*. In the addresses which make up this book he presents a hope for the future — a hope for unity between evangelical churches in the interests of the gospel. That message needs desperately to be heard again.

In 1967, the British Evangelical Council held its first genuinely public conference. Since then, it has met in October or November each year, either in London or in another city of the United Kingdom. The Doctor gave the closing addresses at eight of these conferences between 1967 and 1979 and would have been asked to speak more often on these occasions were it not for ill-health. Indeed, he was scheduled to speak at the Leeds conference in 1976 but, being unwell at the time, was forced to withdraw at short notice.

Roland Lamb, the first full-time and dedicated General Secretary of the Council, deputized for him on that occasion. The following pages contain those addresses in the order in which they were delivered. Inserted among them at the appropriate point is the address on the Mayflower Pilgrims which he gave in Westminster Chapel. This was delivered at a special meeting arranged by the BEC to commemorate the 350th anniversary of the sailing of the Pilgrim Fathers to the New World. Three of the addresses which appear in this book were previously published in booklet form, but they are all now out of print.

The years between 1967-1979 represent a period in which the Doctor was openly and firmly committed to the BEC. He entertained great hopes for it, but was not blind to the difficulties which beset it, as these addresses will show. He was during those years its chief protagonist. This was so much the case that someone coming new to the evangelical scene in England in the late sixties could be forgiven for thinking that the Doctor and the BEC had never been apart and that the Council owed its existence as well as its character to him. That was not so.

The BEC was founded in 1952, not in 1967. Its birthplace was St Columba's Free Church in Edinburgh, and not Westminster Chapel in London. Its founding figures were G. N. M. Collins and Murdoch Macrae of the Free Church of Scotland and T. H. Bendor-Samuel and E. J. Poole-Connor of the Fellowship of Independent Evangelical Churches. They and others were soon joined by W. J. Grier, a minister of the Irish Evangelical Church, which later became the Evangelical Presbyterian Church of Ireland. The World Council of Churches had been constituted four years before in Amsterdam and those who met at Edinburgh were opposed to the ecumenism which it represented. At that time in Edinburgh, Dr Carl McIntyre was attempting to commence a branch of the International Council of Christian Churches in Britain and he was hopeful that the meeting referred to would be the nucleus for that development. However, the decision which was taken was to found what became the BEC, and not a British section of the ICCC. The reason for this decision was that those present did not find the spirit and stance of the ICCC acceptable and they genuinely believed they could do something better. While their aim was to oppose the false ecumenism of the WCC, their great concern was to pursue evangelical unity in a way that was more in keeping with evangelical Christianity in Britain.

It must be recorded that the Doctor was not present at those discussions.

What is perhaps less well known is the surprising fact that when *public* contact was first made between the infant organization and the Doctor, it seemed that they would not come together. Soon after 1952, a luncheon was held in the Cora Hotel in Bloomsbury, London, perhaps in January 1954, to which various evangelical leaders were invited. An account of the origin and purpose of the BEC was given with a view to enlisting the support of those present for its continuance and development. The Doctor was there. When the time came for reactions to the new organization to be expressed, he made it clear that he did not feel he should join in. This must have been a blow to the BEC, given the Doctor's standing even at that time, but he more than made up for it in 1966/7 and until his homecall in 1981. It was the Doctor who put the BEC on the evangelical map; he proclaimed its charter and ran up its flag.

We are therefore faced with an interesting question. How should we account for the change on the Doctor's part between 1952 and 1966/7? As far as one can discover, no record exists of the meeting at the Cora Hotel, or of the reason or reasons which the Doctor gave for withholding his support. Perhaps he gave none. We are therefore in the realm of exploration but not, mercifully, in complete darkness.

There are two things which can be said about the Doctor without fear of being contradicted. These are, that he was not only committed to fearless thought, but also to rethinking. This applied to all but the essentials of Christian orthodoxy, which to him were unassailable. Consequently, whenever facts, whether biblical or scientific, required it, he was not afraid to change his mind and to say so. Many ministers can testify to being force-fed by him with the logical consequences of a position which they had expressed. In this way, they were not only taught to think by him, but also to reflect on their own thinking. But he himself was not immune to his own rigorous logic. One well-known example of this was in connection with the need for an evangelical theological seminary. He acknowledged this at the inauguration of the London Theological Seminary, when he described himself as doubtless appearing to the gathering as 'a poacher turned gamekeeper'. He then said, 'My only defence is that I always try to be open to any conviction produced by the facts.'

Is this, then, the direction in which we must look for an

explanation of the Doctor's change of mind in relation to the BEC? Did he discover new facts, of which he was unaware in 1952, which necessitated what seems to be such a *volte-face* on his part? It is, I believe, impossible to argue this successfully. The evidence against such an explanation is that, in the fifties, he was well aware of the existence and features of the ecumenical threat and was opposed to it; and that he favoured an evangelical unity and argued for it. Addresses which he gave in that decade in England, Scotland and Wales make that abundantly clear. Of particular relevance is the address entitled *Maintaining the Evangelical Faith Today,* which was given as early as 1952. Why, then, did he not join an organization which was opposed to the WCC and in favour of bringing evangelicals together?

Perhaps there is a clue for our enquiry in the word 'organization' which has just been used. The Doctor's opposition to organizations or movements which bypass or sideline churches was formed by the fifties and has since become well known. It is not impossible that this conviction gave him reservations about the BEC. But this cannot be the explanation by itself because of two opposite factors which doubtless would have been made clear at the Cora Hotel meeting, and which one suspects he would have known anyway.

First, the British Committee for Common Evangelical Action (the original name for the BEC) resulted from an approach by one denomination to another group of churches. It was not therefore a case of some individuals 'doing their own thing'. In April 1952, Rev. G. N. M. Collins, acting on behalf of a committee of the Free Church of Scotland, approached the Council of the FIEC with regard to a conference which the International Council of Christian Churches was holding in Edinburgh that year. The FIEC Council responded positively and the result was the BEC. It was therefore church-based in that sense. Secondly, the first declared aim of the BEC was 'to promote in the British Isles a fellowship of evangelical churches and people for mutual encouragement and help in the things of the Lord'. The BEC was therefore not aiming to supplant churches, but to support them and to strengthen links between them. It is difficult to conceive that the Doctor would not have known of these details. The para-church mentality which the Doctor so castigated was not espoused by the infant BEC. The 'organization' explanation does not therefore get us very far in our investigation.

Are there any other factors which could be relevant at this point?

One could be that the BEC, though church-based in the sense described, was not sufficiently rooted in the local church for the Doctor's liking. It was, in effect, as distinct and removed from the life of individual churches as if it had been a para-church organization. Perhaps this is an anachronistic explanation, derived from the seventies rather than the fifties. But, if it is accurate, then the Doctor saw in the fifties what has become in the seventies and eighties the greatest weakness in the standing and support of the BEC—namely its lack of support from local churches whose co-ordinating bodies have decided to join it.

Leaving that possibility out of our reckoning, we turn to something which was very definitely a factor in the BEC in the fifties. It was the relationship between the BEC and the ICCC, which was also founded in 1948 to oppose the WCC. It needs to be asserted that there was never any formal link between the two organizations. As has been mentioned, the BEC was commenced instead of a British branch of the ICCC after discussions with representatives of that body. Even so, there was not a totally clear line of demarcation between the two organizations and it was therefore possible for someone to wonder what path the BEC would tread in the future. Two sets of facts support this construction.

First, there were members of the BEC who were also personal members of the ICCC, namely, E. J. Poole-Connor and also W. J. Grier, whose denomination was actually a member of that organization. Bishop D. A. Thompson of the Free Church of England was also a member of the ICCC and he had been involved in the Edinburgh meeting in 1952.

Secondly, what became the BEC (this new name was adopted in February 1953) did not refuse all co-operation with the ICCC and the latter, in turn, did not give up its attempt to establish links with the BEC. From the very outset, it was resolved that 'In any matter calling for common action between the Committee and the ICCC, the liaison would be effected through the Irish Evangelical Church which is a constituent member of that Council.' In April 1953 it was resolved that 'While no reference has been made in the published constitution of the BEC to the ICCC, we gladly confirm that we much appreciate the liaison we have with that body through the Irish Evangelical Church.'

It will be noticed from these statements that the BEC was placing a distance between itself and the ICCC by means of the use of an intermediary. But the point still holds that perhaps for the Doctor this was not enough of a distinction. If there is anything in this explanation, as far as the Doctor himself was concerned, his tussle with Dr T. T. Shields of Toronto, reported in the first volume of the biography,[1] demonstrates how much he would have wanted to stand apart from the BEC.

The matter of the BEC's relationship with the ICCC was not finally resolved until November 1955 at the earliest, when, after it had declined to sponsor a visit by Dr Carl McIntyre, a letter was received from the Secretary of the English Consultative Committee of the ICCC expressing 'a desire for friendly relations with the BEC and a willingness to work harmoniously' with it. The BEC had succeeded in establishing itself over against the ICCC without becoming embroiled in what would doubtless have been (from one side) a bitter controversy and from the point of view of the gospel, a damaging one.

There is, however, something more to be offered by way of an explanation of the Doctor's decision not to identify himself with the BEC in the fifties. It is not unconnected with what has just been discussed and it can be put in two complementary ways. On the one hand, he may well have thought that the BEC was prematurely conceived and brought to birth. On the other hand, he could well have thought — and probably did — that it would be hindered in achieving its maximum potential because evangelicals had not been presented with the issues which were at stake and therefore had not been given the opportunity to reflect on and come to a conviction about them. This two-sided explanation of the Doctor's decision not to join the BEC just after 1952 is the one which I favour and wish to propose. In support of it, reference may be made to what the Doctor was saying and doing in the decade following 1952.

In the fifties, the Doctor found himself involved in a great fight for 'the defence and confirmation of the gospel'. Though he was not a belligerent person by nature, and never bellicose, he was by no means 'a pressed man' in what he saw, rightly, to be a holy struggle. He could not ignore the assaults which were being made on the gospel which he loved, and loved to preach. In this conflict he was a front-line combatant. But he was also a backroom strategist — a general as well as a footsoldier. He fought with those he led. But in the fight he never shot first and aimed later. He saw the war; the BEC saw a battle — while other evangelicals were asleep. So he blew the trumpet and sought to awaken and summon all who were truly the Lord's to rally to his side.

Though the WCC was formed in 1948 (after a long pre-history because the movement had been interrupted by two world wars) it was in its infancy as an organization. It had yet to install the machinery necessary for the large-scale output with which we have become familiar. The great foe of the fifties was theological liberalism — in the denominations, the theological colleges, universities and the publishing houses. In exposing the essence of liberalism as he proclaimed the gospel, the Doctor knew that he was also attacking the thinking and vision of the WCC, which was merely a symptom of that disease, though a horrid one. He was never one for dealing with symptoms and leaving the disease untreated. So, having made his own diagnosis, he followed his own prescribed method for treating the condition. What he did then paved the way for 1966/7. During the fifties, he served the cause for which the BEC stood, better than it was capable of doing itself. He took on the foe, but on his own ground, which was the preaching of the gospel and not a denunciation of ecumenism.

How, then, did the Doctor and the BEC come together? The answer to that question must begin with the realization that they were never that far apart. Though the Doctor did not commit himself to the BEC in its early years, he was not totally opposed to it. We are informed by one who was actively involved in the formation of the BEC and was present at the Cora Hotel meeting that what the Doctor said on that occasion was that, while the BEC might be right in its aims, he did not feel that he should join. Clearly he had reservations. This fits in with our suggested explanation concerning timing and the importance of achieving maximum effect.

Alongside this, it must be remembered that the Doctor and the BEC men were not on different planets, each circling in its own orbit. At many points their lives touched, and with regularity. There was the almost monthly Westminster Fellowship, the annual Puritan Conference and various gatherings in connection with the Evangelical Alliance, the Evangelical Library and the Evangelical Movement of Wales. There were also his preaching visits, to churches within and without the BEC. In addition, and of great importance as far as a rising generation of ministerial students were concerned, were meetings of the Inter-Varsity and Theological Students' Fellowships. In all these settings, the Doctor exerted a deep and far-reaching influence, highlighting the departure from the truth which was taking place, its effect on the life and witness of the churches and the need for evangelicals to stand together in its defence and for its dissemination.

Changing the perspective, it is now possible to argue that the Doctor and the BEC men were on converging tracks and not parallel lines. It was the providence of God, unfolding itself in the course of events in the sixties, which brought him to them in an open and public manner. It was his ministry to them which enlarged and sharpened their thinking, recognizing the propriety of a critical stance, but assigning it only a limited place in the broader concern for the spread of the gospel, the unity of the churches and the need for revival. He was educating a generation of evangelicals with regard to the crisis which was developing and how it should be dealt with. Those who stood with him in 1966/7 and stayed with him subsequently were those whom he had been guiding in the preceding years.

The two volumes of addresses to which reference has been made contain striking and notable examples of this teaching. Of particular importance in the period between 1952 and 1966 are the following:

The Puritans
1962 — Puritan perplexities — Some lessons from 1640-1662.
(The Evangelical Library Lecture for 1962 should be read along with this. Its title is 'From Puritanism to Non-Conformity'.)
1963 — John Owen on schism.
1965 — *Ecclesiola in Ecclesia.*

Knowing The Times
1952 — Maintaining the evangelical faith today.
1954 — A policy appropriate to biblical faith.
1959 — Conversions: psychological and spiritual.
1961 — How can we see a return to the Bible?
1962 — The basis of Christian unity.
1963 — Consider your ways.
1964 — The weapons of our warfare.

The first mention of the Doctor in the BEC records is in connection with its Executive meeting of August 1959. For some time consideration had been given to the production of needed literature and the possibility of the Doctor's being asked to produce a pamphlet on the subject of revival was discussed. (At this time the Doctor was preaching a series of sermons on that subject in Westminster Chapel to mark the centenary of the 1859 Revival.) By the end of 1959, the request for a pamphlet was changed to one for permission to print one of his sermons. In March 1960 it was a sermon from the *Westminster Record* on the subject of the inspiration of the Bible which was being sought. In January 1961 a minute records that 'action was still to be taken' on this matter. Whether this means that permission had not been requested, or had not been given, or that publication had not resulted, it is difficult to say. Each of these is a real possibility

In 1964 the Scottish Evangelical Fellowship — an organization made up of the Scottish Evangelical Council, Scottish Reformation Society and the Protestant Institute of Scotland — held a meeting at which the Doctor spoke. This fellowship was very like the BEC in its general stance and it had resolved to use the BEC as its channel for relations with bodies outside Scotland. The significant detail for our purpose is that representatives of the BEC were invited for tea and to share in the evening meeting. Then, on 6 October 1966, two weeks before the crucial meeting at the Westminster Central Hall, the BEC Executive was giving consideration to arranging a London conference and the Doctor was figuring prominently in their thinking.

In January 1967 — after the meeting at the Central Hall — this BEC Executive minute appears: 'It was reported that the old Westminster Fellowship had been terminated by the chairman, Dr D. M. Lloyd-Jones. An enquiry had been made as to the possibility of a new fraternal coming under the aegis of the BEC.' It is not stated who made this enquiry but, as recorded, it is impossible to conceive of its being made without the Doctor's knowledge. This is perhaps the first formal approach of the Doctor to the BEC. By the end of March 1967 two things had occurred. First, the Doctor had spoken at a rally held by the BEC in Plumstead, South London, to draw attention to the decision of the Greater London Council to provide land for the purposes of Christian worship only for an ecumenical centre. Secondly, plans which the BEC had made for a public conference to be held in May had been cancelled. In their place, a public conference in London on 31 October/1 November was being looked to, but it was decided that arrangements for that were only to be made 'after consultation with Dr M. Lloyd-Jones as chairman of the newly formed fellowship of ministers meeting at Westminster'. Clearly the Doctor was now very much involved in the work and witness of the BEC and his stance and powerful influence were recognized by it.

This would therefore be an appropriate point at which to move on to the first address that the Doctor gave at a BEC public conference. But one other matter must be mentioned first. It concerns the address which he gave at the Second National Assembly of Evangelicals in the Central Hall, Westminster on 18 October 1966. Though this assembly was called by the Evangelical Alliance, a strong case could be made for including what he said there in this volume of BEC addresses, had it not already appeared in print. The argument for doing so would be that the Central Hall address is, from the standpoint of concern, thought and vision, the forerunner of the BEC addresses. In it there are references to the distinctiveness of evangelicalism, its tendency to form movements instead of focusing on the importance of the church; the challenge presented to it by the ecumenical developments and yet the opportunity before it; its proneness to be defensive and denominational; its contentment with a 'paper' church and refusal to face up to what the New Testament declared a church really to be. He referred to the danger of exalting doctrinal matters which were secondary to the gospel and the failure to realize the seriousness of apostasy and schism. His concern was that evangelicals should seize the initiative and boldly pursue it, as the Reformers had done, looking to the Holy Spirit to bless a 'fellowship or association of evangelical churches'.

A summary of this address was printed along with the other papers which were presented at the assembly, in a volume entitled *Unity in Diversity*. This symposium appeared in June 1967. In its foreword, written by A. Morgan Derham, the then General Secretary of the Evangelical Alliance, and in the preamble to the summary, two important facts are recorded.

Firstly, the Doctor had been interviewed by the Commission on Church Unity which had been set up following the 1965 assembly.

Secondly, he had been asked by the 'council', not the 'commission', specifically 'to say in public at the rally what he had said in private when speaking to them'.[2]

In spite of this acknowledgement, an inaccurate and unjust report has been put about and gained credence. It was presented in the

February 1990 issue of *Christianity Today* in an article on English evangelicalism. It was declared there that what the Doctor said at the Central Hall was something which took the council of the Evangelical Alliance and the chairman of the meeting completely by surprise. But what was worse was that the Doctor had been invited to speak on unity and had spoken instead on separation. A reading of the address in *Knowing the Times* and the relevant section of the biography ³ will not only confirm the account in *Unity and Diversity* but also serve to indicate that the Dcotor did speak on unity, not separation. It all depends, of course, on what is understood by *church* unity!

In order to try and settle this matter once and for all and to provide a context for the addresses in this book, I quote the opening of the address in question.

The Doctor began as follows: 'My subject is church unity, and I am speaking on this at the request of the Commission to which reference has been made. I think that is important, lest anybody should think that I am taking advantage of the kindness and generosity of the authorities in inviting me to speak here tonight, to foist my own views upon you. I had the privilege of being called as a witness to appear before this Commission and I made a statement of my attitude with regard to these matters. It was the members of the Commission themselves who asked me to state in public here tonight what I am now proposing to say to you. So it is really their responsibility. They have already heard it, and they asked me to repeat it to you.'

The Doctor then continued: 'But I am not apologizing for this. I am very glad indeed of the opportunity because I believe we are considering tonight what is incomparably the most important question that Christian people can be considering and facing at this present time. Had I my way, I would have given the whole of this conference to this one subject... I believe that [it] is the key to the solution of all our other problems.'

What was the Doctor referring to? It was 'church unity'. This he identified with 'evangelical ecumenicity'. He called on his fellow evangelicals to place the church before alliances or societies, as the New Testament would have them do; to recognize that they were guilty of the sin of schism, for only those who were one on the essentials of salvation could commit that sin; and to come together, not occasionally while maintaining a union with those who denied the gospel, but permanently 'as a fellowship, or an association, of evangelical churches'.

It is worth pointing out that not once in this address did the Doctor use the terms 'separate/secede'. His call was to *associate* or *unite*. While it is granted that this necessarily involved secession, the basis of the call was the gospel, the scope of the call was to those who professsed to believe the gospel and the purpose in view was the spread of the gospel. It was therefore neither schismatic nor exclusivist, but truly Christian and evangelical. In addition, as the Doctor pointed out, it was timely because in the wider setting denominational attachments were being questioned and new alignments were being considered. Should not evangelicals, of all people, take up the challenge, notwithstanding the difficulties, and seize the opportunity to stand together for God's truth?

This address, as is well known, met with an immediate negative reaction. The positive response surfaced later, most noticeably in the Luther meeting. On 1 November 1967 over 2,500 people gathered in Westminster Chapel to commemorate the 450th anniversary of Luther's promulgation of his Ninety-Five Theses. The top gallery of the chapel, which was supposed to be closed, was more full than empty before the overflow was accommodated in an extension hall. The Doctor confessed himself to be 'immensely encouraged' by the great number who were 'not ashamed of the Protestant Reformation'. Luther had been mentioned in the Central Hall address as an example of 'all the martyrs and confessors throughout the ages who had not been deterred by difficulties as they responded to the truth'. This address summoned the congregation to a like faith.

So we come to the addresses themselves. They deal with questions which are not only central to the matter of unity, whether of the ecumenical or evangelical kind, but also to the quality, strength and usefulness of true faith and to the preservation and propagation of authentic Christianity. They are reproduced with a minimum of editing, as the Doctor would have wished.

Though a decade or so has passed since the last address was given, their relevance has increased rather than diminished. The termination of the British Council of Churches (31 August 1990) and its replacement by the Council of Churches of Britain and Ireland, in which the Roman Catholic Church is stately involved, has made the ecumenical threat more formidable and widespread than ever before. Yet, more evangelical churches and leaders are involved in it now than in 1979. The rejection of *evangelical* unity in 1966 has become an adoption of *ecumenical* unity in 1991. May the publication of these addresses, therefore, have an even greater effect than when they were actually delivered. Their appearance in time for the fortieth anniversary of the founding of the BEC is most opportune, because in many of them the Doctor was presenting an apologia for the existence and purpose of the BEC. It is still the case that the BEC is the only body of churches in the United Kingdom which 'cannot, on grounds of conscience, identify with that ecumenicity which lacks an evangelical basis'. It takes this position because it stands for the unity of all those churches which believe the one and only gospel which saves.

1. Iain Murray, *D. Martyn Lloyd-Jones, The First Forty Years, 1899-1939*, Banner of Truth Trust, pp. 271-4.

2. *Unity in Diversity*, p.8.

3. Iain Murray, *D. Martyn Lloyd-Jones, The Fight of Faith, 1939-1981*, Banner of Truth Trust, pp. 522-32.

2.
Luther and his message for today

Two elements in this address call for highlighting.

First, a development from the 1966 Central Hall address is evident. Instead of a positive call to evangelicals to unite in an association of evangelical churches, this address led up to an explicit call to them to secede from denominations which were moving towards Rome by their involvement in the ecumenical movement.

Secondly, the Doctor used the expression 'guilt by association' in this address. It is important to examine this in its context, both historically and in the address itself, and to avoid reacting unthinkingly to what became an emotive slogan. By these words the Doctor was not advocating what has become known as 'second degree separation' and treading the sectarian path. His concern was still for gospel unity. What he was doing was questioning those who, in the previous twelve highly charged months , had repeatedly rejected a call to gospel unity in favour of a denominational loyalty which countenanced serious error. When the relevant passage in the address, which is the wording agreed with the Doctor himself, is read carefully ,it can be seen that he was not in fact charging anyone wth guilt, but putting an important question to those in the doctrinally mixed denominations who would be 'content to function' in the same church as those 'who deny the very elements of the Christian faith'.

Those who were present at this meeting will never forget the occasion.

I was very concerned that something should be done in London to celebrate this great and important occasion which we are calling to mind [the publication of Luther's Ninety-five Theses]. My subject is: 'Luther and his message for today.' I confess freely that I am immensely encouraged at the sight of this congregation. I have a feeling that you have come together to demonstrate, to make a declaration, which is, that unlike so many others at this present time you are not ashamed of the Protestant Reformation. There are many people today who are ashamed of it. There are many who keep quiet about it. It is very interesting to have observed that the secular press has appeared to take a greater interest in this than has the Christian church in this country. We can well understand that. The ecclesiastical leaders are afraid of calling attention to Luther and the Reformation because they have ideas in their minds, and plans and purposes which they are putting into execution, which are travelling in the exact opposite direction. So, as one who knows at times what it is to understand the feelings of Elijah under the juniper tree on that famous occasion, I am glad to find that, if not exactly 7,000, there are at any rate some 2,500 and more who have not bowed the knee to Baal. I am immensely encouraged, and I feel sure that the same applies to all of you.

Now this great event which we are commemorating, the first step which led eventually to the Protestant Reformation, is not something to be hidden. It was not done in a corner, and it has made itself known in the history of the world ever since. It is something to glory in; it is something to boast of. And if you and I are true followers of Martin Luther and the Reformation, well, we must thank God for his exceeding grace to his people at that time.

A turning-point of history

This is an event and occasion which merits attention and commemoration for many, many reasons. Quite apart from the great religious reason that brings us together tonight, everybody has to admit that Luther's action in 1517 has changed the entire course of history. The historians are granting that and, as I say, the secular newspapers are granting that history has been different ever since, and you really cannot understand what is generally called modern history apart from the Reformation. You cannot understand the history of this country, you cannot understand, especially, the history of the United States of America. There would never have been Pilgrim Fathers if there had not been a Protestant Reformation. So you see it has been something very vital in connection with the whole history of the human race.

Not only that, it has affected profoundly the modern view of politics and of law. Prior to the Reformation the church generally governed politics; she controlled emperors and kings and potentates, and governed the law of lands. All that has been changed.

But not only that, it has changed literature. It is very true to say that Martin Luther in a sense created the German language as it has been known to us, and you cannot understand literature in general, particularly German literature, apart from him.

And when you come even to the realm of science it is being granted generally by modern historians that you would never have had modern science were it not for the Reformation. All scientific investigation and endeavour prior to that had been controlled by the church. There was no liberty of investigation, and any conclusions men might arrive at which did not tally with the philosophy, the Aristotelian and Thomist philosophy, controlling the thinking of the church, were rejected. It is the Protestant Reformation that led to liberty for scientific investigation. It is just sheer ignorance of history that makes many a modern scientist regard Protestantism and the true evangelical faith as being something that is opposed to true science.

I could go on telling you of other effects that this great event has had on the history of mankind. Perhaps nothing is more important than the way it brought to the forefront the sovereignty of the individual conscience. Now I know that things happened at that time, and things were done by Luther, that seem to militate against this. Nevertheless his fundamental teaching laid down once and for ever the right of the individual to his conscience, and his right to follow the dictates of his conscience. So many men who talk lightly and glibly about 'liberty' do not know, and do not realize, that they owe what they are enjoying to this great event.

What is it, then, that we are trying to remember together? We are going to look at an event which took place 450 years ago. Most authorities would say that it happened on October 31st. It was the occasion when Martin Luther nailed the Ninety-five Theses on the door of the Castle Church at Wittenberg. But there are historical authorities who argue — and it seems to me with a considerable degree of cogency — that the actual date was November 1st.

Well, what was it that happened? What happened was that a man took ninety-five propositions, or theses, and nailed them to the door of that church. Now the door of the church, in those days, was used as we now use notice-boards. You know how in any university or college there is always a notice-board, and if you want to call attention to something you put a notice up on the notice-board. That is exactly what this man did — he nailed his Ninety-five Theses or propositions to the door of that particular church in order that he might call attention to what he was saying in them, and in order that that might lead to a public disputation concerning these matters. He was primarily addressing his fellow members of the faculty of the university, but he was also addressing anybody else who had the ability to understand what he was saying. He had written them in Latin, and they were meant primarily and most essentially as a kind of academic discussion.

Who was this man? His name was Martin Luther. He was a monk, he was a lecturer also in theology, and he was a preacher — he was pre-eminently, perhaps, a preacher. At that time he was thirty-four years of age. What was he doing? What was his object? It is very important that we should realize that he was not setting out to break with the church of Rome. That was not in his mind at all at that time. Indeed he was most anxious not to do that. I am making a point of this for a reason that will emerge later on. He said, 'No crime or abuse can justify a schism.' It is not surprising that he said that. He was speaking out of a background of some twelve centuries of the rigid Roman Catholic system and the idea of the one church. All he was proposing to do was to call attention to a grave scandal that was taking place at that time in the church in connection with what was called 'the sale of indulgences'. That is all he proposed to do. But nevertheless, in doing that, he was unconsciously taking the first step that led eventually to the Protestant Reformation, and to the formation of a new church, the Protestant church.

The matter of indulgences

What was this question of indulgences? What was causing Luther such concern? Well, indulgences meant this — they were certificates given under the authority of the pope which allowed people not to carry out the full penalty that had been imposed upon them because of their sins. This was a system that had gradually come into being in the church in connection with what the Roman Catholic Church calls 'the sacrament of penance'. When a man fell into sin, at first it was the church in general that decided what form his penance should take. He had to do certain things to atone, as it were, for his sin; he had to bear a certain punishment, and the church decided what it was. But the church had the power, if it chose, later on to remit a certain portion of the sentence, and that was called an 'indulgence'.

Now at first this was done by the church in general, but after a while the power to do this was taken from the church and was taken over by the priests only. They took it from the people, as they took so many other things, and they said they alone had a right to do this. But, of course, that had not gone on very long before the pope came in and said that this was really his prerogative. So it was taken even out of the hands of the priests into the hands of the pope himself. This was the idea, that the priests had power to give a man absolution for his sins, but though a man had had absolution he still had to bear certain consequences of his sins in this world and, indeed, even in the next world. At that point they introduced their doctrine of purgatory, which says that even the souls of the redeemed have to go to this place they call purgatory and there endure certain elements and aspects of the punishment of their sins, and then they gradually work through that and eventually go to paradise.

So indulgences, you see, came to mean this — that the pope had it within his power to shorten or to lessen the punishment that those whose sins had been absolved should suffer in this world and also in the next world in purgatory. The pope claimed that he had this power to do this, and he said that he had got this power because there was in the possession of the church a great accumulation of right-eousness. Where had this come from? Well, they taught that it had come partly from the Lord Jesus Christ himself, but they taught that in addition it had come from the lives of saints in the church. They taught that these saints had lived such good lives that they had not only done sufficient, and produced sufficient righteousness to cover themselves, they had produced a superabundance of righteousness. This was called their work of 'supererogation'. So the church had accumulated in this way a great reserve of grace, as it were, which was in the charge of the pope, and he could give of that to anybody whom he chose. He did so by giving a 'certificate of indulgence'.

Now that is the real meaning of this term 'indulgence'. The pope sometimes did this for nothing; but not very often! He generally did it on the payment of a fee. It really began and became quite a business in connection with the Crusaders. Any man who took part in the Crusades was automatically given an indulgence. But after the end of the Crusades it was gradually extended to other people, and so it became eventually something that anyone could obtain on the payment of a fee.

The price paid varied tremendously; it varied from half a florin to twenty-five florins. And this is where the real scandal came in that led to the action of Luther. As the years passed this practice became more and more of a scandal, but it really became acute in 1507. Luther, remember, was born in 1483. In 1507 Pope Julius II decided to rebuild the famous church of St Peter's in Rome, and it was to be done magnificently. If you have ever been there you will have seen it, and you will have seen how magnificently it was done from the artistic point of view. So, naturally, it cost a tremendous lot of money. In order to help to defray the cost the pope decided that he would issue a great mass of indulgences. He allocated that given amounts should be gathered in this way, by the payment of indulgences, in different parts of the world. In that part of Germany in which Luther lived the sum allocated for collection for the rebuilding of St Peter's was 52,000 florins. This obviously meant that the business arrangements had to be worked out very thoroughly.

There was a man who had become archbishop twice over at the age of twenty-three, a man of the name of Albert of Mainz. Of course he had to pay for these great offices, and to borrow from a famous banking firm in order to pay the pope for them. So an arrangement was arrived at between the pope and the bankers, the Fuggers, and this man Albert, twice-over archbishop, that half the money collected for the payment of indulgences should go to Rome to rebuild St Peter's, and that the other half was to be divided between Albert himself and the bankers to whom he was in debt. A notorious man of the name of Tetzel was appointed to go round preaching, and preaching indulgences, and telling the people of the wonderful bargains they could have. Among many other things which he said was this, that 'souls leaped from the flames of purgatory as the florins rattled into his coffer'. He went even beyond that and had the effrontery and the arrogance to say that, even if a man had committed a foul sexual assault upon the Virgin Mary, he could get an indulgence if he paid the appropriate fee.

All this had become a terrible scandal, and in particular in this part of Germany where Luther lived. So Luther was constantly meeting this problem. He could see that the people were relying on this system of indulgences for forgiveness of sins. He was concerned as a pastor and as a preacher. He could see that the people were being deluded.

However, it all came to a crisis in this way. There was a great festival to be held in Wittenberg, where Luther lived and taught. The festival was in connection with a kind of exhibition of relics that was held periodically by the Elector of Saxony, under whose jurisdiction Luther lived. He claimed to have relics of the cross and of various other things. He used to have this kind of exhibition of relics, and it was to be held on this November 1st, 1517. Luther knew that people would be coming from all directions, for they could get indulgences even for visiting the relics. But at the same time he knew that many of the people would be travelling to listen to the preaching of this terrible man Tetzel. Luther was disturbed in his soul, and it was this that really led him to nail his Ninety-five Theses to the door. He said that something must be done about this scandal, this offence in the church.

Let me again emphasize that that was really his motive at that point; he wanted primarily to call attention to, and to correct, this terrible abuse. We have got to be accurate and true to the facts, so I have to remind you that Luther at that time, at that point, did not object to indulgences as such. As a Roman Catholic, one brought up in Catholicism, he believed in indulgences, as long as they were administered in the right way. So his whole object, at this point, was not so much to attack the church as a whole, nor her teaching, but to correct this terrible abuse in connection with this matter of indulgences. And yet — and this is the thing that is so interesting for us and from which I trust we shall learn certain lessons together — though his primary object was to deal with and to correct the abuses in connection with the indulgences, he did that in such a way that inevitably it led to the general reformation of doctrine and, eventually, separation from the Roman church.

The Ninety-five Theses

But before I come to deal with that, let me just give some indication of the character of these theses. This is the introduction to what he nailed up on the door: 'Out of love and zeal for truth, and the desire to bring it to light, the following theses will be publicly discussed at Wittenberg under the chairmanship of the Rev. Father Martin Luther, Master of Arts and Sacred Theology, and regularly appointed lecturer on these subjects at that place. He requests that those who cannot be present to debate orally with us will do so by letter.' That is his introduction. Then follow the Ninety-five Theses. They are quite short. I only wish I had time to quote them all, for they are fascinating; I am going to pick out some of the more interesting ones.

Here is the first — and you observe how, in the very first thesis, his theology comes through. Here it is: 'When our Lord and Master Jesus Christ said, "Repent," he willed the entire life of believers to be one of repentance.' You see, the teaching of indulgences — that once you have paid your money and got your indulgence, all was well, that you had finished your repentance as far as that was concerned, at any rate — is attacked directly. He throws down the gauntlet in the very first thesis: 'When our Lord and Master Jesus Christ said, "Repent," he willed the entire life of believers to be one of repentance.'

Or take *number 32*, which is another interesting one: 'Those who believe that they can be certain of their salvation because they have indulgence letters will be eternally damned, together with their teachers.'

Now, remember, he was not really setting out to deal with theological issues; yet in spite of that, you see, it comes out.

No. 36: 'Any truly repentant Christian has a right to full remission of penalty and guilt even without indulgence letters.' What an attack on the pope, without intending to do it!

Then let us go on to *number 37*: 'Any true Christian, whether living or dead, participates in all the blessings of Christ and the church, and this is granted him by God even without indulgence letters.' He is rubbing it home, is he not?

No. 45: 'Christians are to be taught that he who sees a needy man and passes him by, yet gives his money for indulgences, does not buy papal indulgences but God's wrath.' And they were doing that. They felt that they must have forgiveness, and believed it could be bought in this way. So instead of giving their money to some pauper or starving person, they took the money and paid it in order to get the indulgences. That is his comment upon that practice.

No. 46: 'Christians are taught that, unless they have more than they need, they must reserve enough for their family needs and by no means squander it on indulgences.' This is what people today would call 'strong stuff', is it not? And yet, remember, his concern was to correct abuses.

But let us go on.

No. 62: 'The true treasure of the church is the most holy gospel of the glory and grace of God.' He is preaching to the pope at this point. This is 'the true treasure of the church', not some supposed accumulated treasure as the result of the work of supererogation of the saints, and so on.

No. 75: 'To consider papal indulgences so great that they could absolve a man even if he had done the impossible and had violated the Mother of God is madness.' I quoted that just now; there he puts it quite plainly.

But let me come to the last ones, *numbers 92 and 95*: 'Away then with all those prophets who say to the people of Christ, "Peace, peace", and there is no peace.'

'Away with those prophets who say to the people of Christ, "Cross, Cross", and there is no cross!'

'Christians', says number 94, 'should be exhorted to be diligent in following Christ, their Head, through penalties, death and hell; and thus be confident of entering into heaven through many tribulations rather than through the false security of peace.' 'The false security of peace,' of course, means the peace that these poor ignorant people obtained as the result of paying their money in order to obtain these indulgences.

That, then, is the thing that we are actually celebrating — the nailing of these Ninety-five Theses to that door at Wittenberg for discussion amongst the faculty. But, as I have been showing you, something deeper kept on creeping through. These propositions, which were primarily meant to deal solely with indulgences, contained something else, something deeper, something bigger — that something that in a sense 'sparked off' the Protestant Reformation. What was it?

Luther's spiritual pilgrimage

Here, to me, is the thing that is most fascinating. The answer is, the story of the spiritual pilgrimage of this mighty man, Martin Luther.

He was born on November 10th, 1483. He was a young man of great
abilities, so his poor father put him to the study of law, intending him
to be a lawyer. And he might very well have been a lawyer, were it
not that on a certain day in the year 1505 he was very nearly killed
by a thunderbolt that struck him to the ground during a terrifying
thunderstorm. He was terrified, and he prayed saying, 'Help me, St
Anne!' He was a Roman Catholic, remember, so he prayed, 'Help
me, St Anne, and I will become a monk!' He came face to face with
death, and he was not ready for it. He was terrified and convicted
deeply, and he never forgot it. In a sense the Protestant Reformation
starts with a thunderbolt!

You remember the story of the conversion of the Philippian jailer
in Acts 16 and the part played in it by an earthquake! You know, my
friends, when the world becomes so mad that it will not listen to the
preaching of the gospel, God has got other ways of calling attention
to the truth. A thunderbolt or an earthquake! What will this generation, to which you and I belong, have to meet, I wonder? But let
us take heart, brethren; whatever they may do with us as preachers,
God reigns, and he rules the thunder and the lightning and the storms
and the wind. This man was struck to the ground, and the great
process of reformation began as the result of a thunderbolt.

The result of this was that he became a monk and entered an
Augustinian monastery at Erfurt, and was under a very great man
called Staupitz who played quite a part in his life. I have not the time
to tell you the story fully; I am picking out the salient features. In
1507 he celebrated his first 'mass', as they called it, and still call it.
But the very act of doing that got him into spiritual trouble. He felt
that he was unworthy to do this. Who was he to offer what he thought
was the body of Christ? Who was he? Who was he to approach this
God to whom he was making the offering? He was troubled about
this, he was unhappy about his soul. In 1508 he was sent to the
University of Wittenberg. Staupitz felt that Luther was an intellectual, and that it would be good for him, perhaps, to go to the
university and there engage his great mind, and get rid of what he
regarded partly as a kind of morbidity and a tendency to introspec-
tion. In 1510 he visited Rome.

There are stories about that visit, but one gathers from the
historians that we must not believe all the legends that we have been
accustomed to — it does not matter. His conversion certainly did not
take place in Rome in 1510. In 1512 he was made the prior of an

Augustinian priory, and at the same time he was appointed lecturer
or professor in theology. But during the whole of this time he had a
great problem, and this was it: 'How can I find a gracious God?' He
knew the righteousness and the justice of God; he knew of the terrors
of God's law but — how can I find a gracious God? This was his
problem. How can I get assurance of forgiveness of my sins?

An authority has put it like this: 'What Luther really cared about
from 1505 to 1515 was not the reform of the church, it was Luther,
the soul of Luther, the salvation of Luther — nothing more.' It was
intensely personal. Here was a man under conviction of sin and who
could not find peace. Here was a man looking for forgiveness, and
nobody could tell him how to obtain it. This caused the agony of his
soul all these years. His teacher, Staupitz, advised him to read the
mystics, and he did so. He read the works of St Bernard. He read the
sermons of a great preacher that had appeared in Germany of the
name of Tauler. He read a wonderful little volume — it was the first
thing that he ever reprinted — called *Theologia Germanica (German Theology)* — a kind of mystical theology. You can still get it.
He read this, and it did something for him; and for a while he thought
this was going to be the way out. But after a while he saw that he
would never find peace by way of mysticism. He had already seen
that he could not obtain it by his own works, but he found now that
mysticism also is a very subtle form of works. Under its teaching he
had to strive for self-surrender, and that is a most terrible task. To try
to surrender your self, or to get rid of your self, is very much more
difficult even than the performance of external acts of righteousness. So he saw that mysticism left it all with him again; he was
striving and struggling for this self-surrender and absorption in God,
and he could not do it.

So he came back again to the Bible; and this is the fascinating
thing about him. He lets us know that it was his very preparation of
his lectures for his students, and his sermons for the people, that
really brought him to see the truth. His own preparation was the very
means used by God for his conviction. From 1513 to 1516 he
lectured on the Psalms; from 1515 and 1516 he lectured on the
epistle to the Romans; and as he studied this and was preparing for
it the truth very slowly began to dawn upon him.

Another factor also came in. There had been a revival of interest
in the writings of the great St Augustine. It had started about 1509;
and Luther, like others, began to read his works. He read *The*

Confessions of St Augustine, he read his famous two volumes, *The City of God,* he read him on *True Religion and Christian Doctrine,* he read him also on the Psalms and on Romans. In preparing his own lectures he wondered whether Augustine could help him, so he turned to Augustine on the Psalms and on the epistle to the Romans, and gradually he began to understand and to believe Augustine's teaching on justification by faith. It was not what Luther himself taught later; it was not what you and I believe; but he did see the principle, at any rate, of justification by faith. There was error mixed up with it, but in essence he seems to have got hold of it.

Another thing that helped him was that Erasmus, that great scholar and humanist, had produced his edition of the New Testament in Greek in 1516. All these things together helped Luther. But it is very wrong to say, as I read in the leading article, I think it was in the *Baptist Times,* that the Reformation really is the outcome of the Renaissance. It is not. It helped a little, in producing this good text and in stimulating thought in general, but as Luther himself said, 'It is very certain that neither study nor intelligence can give us insight into Holy Writ. There is no master interpreter of the divine words except the Author of the Word.' The Renaissance and Erasmus gave a certain amount of help, but they were not the means of bringing Luther right through to the truth.

Well, here he is: he is beginning to see the truth; his own studies of the Psalms and of the epistle to the Romans are bringing him nearer and nearer to this great saving doctrine of justification by faith. But it took a particular experience to bring him to it. He had that experience in the tower of the monastery in which he lived. It is referred to generally as 'the tower experience'.

Luther's conversion

There is much argument as to when this happened. I have gone into this as best I can and I am quite satisfied that it happened before this important event in 1517 when he nailed his theses to the church door. This is how he puts it. There he was in this tower; he was reading, he was meditating, he was praying. 'I laboured diligently and anxiously as to how to understand Paul's word in Romans 1:17, where he says, "The righteousness of God is revealed in the gospel". I sought long and knocked anxiously, for the expression "the righteousness of God" blocked the way. As often as I read that declaration I wished always that God had not made the gospel known.' He interpreted that phrase, you see, as meaning the righteousness that God demands of us, a righteousness that we have got to produce; and this, he said, 'blocked the way'; he could not do it. So he says, 'I wished that God had not made that declaration, and that the gospel had not been made known.' Then he goes on, 'But, once when I was meditating in the tower of the monastery in Wittenberg, when I saw the difference, that law is one thing and gospel another, I broke through, and as I had formerly hated the expression "the righteousness of God", I now began to regard it as my dearest and most comforting word, so that this expression of Paul's became to me in very truth a gate to paradise.'

What had he seen? Well, what he had seen was this — that 'the righteousness of God' in Romans 1:17 is not a righteousness that you and I have to create, and attain unto, or buy by means of indulgences; it is a righteousness that God gives us; it is a righteousness that he 'clothes' us with; it is the free gift of God by grace through faith, the righteousness of God by faith: 'The just shall live by faith.' He 'broke through' he says, and this expression which had so terrified him became now his 'dearest and most comforting word, so that this expression of Paul's became to me in very truth a gate to paradise'.

All those emphases to which I drew your attention in the theses were the result of that. He had come to see this vital central truth. This is the way of forgiveness and yet, as he knew so well, the people believed that they could buy it, that it was in the gift of the pope, and from him the gift of the priests. He now knew that this was entirely wrong. This knowledge was working in him unconsciously. It was the scandal in connection with the sale of the indulgences that drew his attention, and yet behind it he was really questioning and querying the whole notion of indulgences, the whole idea of penance, indeed the whole question of the way of salvation as taught by the church. But it was not his intention to do this. He simply put up the theses to get a discussion on the scandals.

What happened? Well, he sent a copy to the Elector of Saxony where he lived, but God was in this. Other people got hold of these theses, which were in Latin; they translated them into German and they printed them; and in a few weeks hundreds of copies of these theses were available. It spread like wildfire; it became a best seller.

He never intended that, and at first he was really quite annoyed about it. But whatever he might think about it, that is what happened.

And then, of course, he was attacked by Tetzel. He was reported to his superiors, reported to the archbishop — he had sent a copy of it to him — and he was eventually reported to the pope. The result of this was that he had to appear on trial several times. He had discussions with a famous debater called Eck. But this is what happened: the more they tried to criticize his theses, and the more they attacked him, the more they drove him back to the Bible, the more certain he became of his ground, and he saw these great doctrines more and more clearly. So that their very opposition by 1519 made him write this, that 'The pope is veritable Antichrist'. Eventually he came to see that the entire Roman Catholic system was opposed to the gospel, and completely wrong.

I want to emphasize that this was something that happened to him gradually. He did not see it all in a sudden flash. He did have this flash in connection with justification by faith, but not about all these other doctrines. He went on from step to step. He says himself, 'Like Augustine, I was one of those who progressed by writing and by teaching.' His very preparation, as I say, convinced himself: 'I did not learn my theology at a single stroke, I had to bury myself in it ever more deeply.' His oft-repeated phrase was, 'God led me on.' Eventually by 1520 — which was one of his great years, and in which he published a number of his most important works that are still available for us to read — he had really seen all the great fundamental evangelical principles of the Christian faith and they were clear to him.

He was not only interested in the speculative features of theology, he was always interested primarily in God's holiness, God's love, man's sinfulness, law, gospel, Christ, faith, justification. And all this brought him on to see the centrality of the Scriptures and that the Scriptures alone are our authority. *'Sola Scriptura'* — not the tradition, not the teaching of the church. In the various disputations that he had his opponents were always quoting the teaching of the church and the councils and tradition, but he kept on saying, 'What does the Word say? What does the Scripture say?' He was always bringing them back to the Word. Tradition and the teaching of the church, he said, are not equal to the Scriptures; the Scriptures alone are our authority.

Furthermore, he asserted that the church is not the sole

interpreter of the Scriptures. The Roman church had taught that, and she still teaches that. You know that the Roman church is now encouraging her people to buy Bibles and read them; but she is very careful to tell them that she alone can interpret them truly and authoritatively. She was saying it then; she is still saying it. Luther, on the other hand, said that any man with the Spirit in him can read and understand the Scriptures. He began to assert the universal priesthood of all believers; he rejected the division into clergy and laity, saying that there is no such thing. He said that a poor serving girl sweeping a room with a brush is in as good a position as the pope himself, if necessary, to understand these things, if she has got the Spirit. He did away with monks and orders and all these false institutions that had come into the life of the church.

At the same time he came to see the true view with regard to the sacraments. 'Sacraments', he said, 'do not act in and of themselves — *"ex opere operato"*.' They are not magical, they do not act in and of themselves. He said that there is no such thing as the 'mass'. This was a figment of the imagination, the creation of men. At the same time he denounced the doctrine of transubstantiation. Now all this had happened by 1520. He put a great deal of it into a book which he called *The Babylonian Captivity of the Church.*

Luther the man

There is the history in its essence, necessarily incomplete owing to lack of time. We are here, however, to call attention first and foremost to Luther and that action which he took in nailing the theses to the door of the church in Wittenberg. It is right to praise famous men. There is a kind of piety that seems to think that this is wrong. I dissent from that completely. Martin Luther is worth looking at. Would that there were more like him at the present time. God uses men. Do not forget that. He produces the men, as I am going to show you, and they are very wonderful men. Luther was a wonderful man, and it is worth our while to have a look at him for a moment. He was an outstanding genius. There is no other word that can describe him. He was not only able, he was a genius.

The next thing that strikes us about him is his honesty, his scrupulous honesty. Then, his amazing courage. There are those who say — and I think they are quite right — that if he had not been

led along the way he was by God he probably would have been one
of the great musicians of all time. He certainly was very fond of
music. He was not very interested in art, but he was passionately
fond of music, and he could compose music, as you know. The only
word I find that is adequate to describe this man is this — he was a
volcano. He was a great mountain of a man, but he was a mountain
on fire; and he erupted and threw out the most precious things. It is
true to add that he also threw out a lot of dross. It is right, as I say,
to look at men, but when we do so truly, and when we face all the
facts, we see that the best men are fallible. But he was God's man
for this occasion and therefore the right man.

Others before Luther had said many of the things that he said. Let
us not forget in this country that John Wycliffe has said many of
them, and John Wycliffe had influenced a man called John Hus long
before Luther. And yet, you see, these men did not lead to this great
Reformation. Why not? Well, Luther, I think, answers the question.
'John Hus,' he says, 'attacked and castigated only the the pope's evil
and scandalous life, but I have attacked the pope's doctrine and
overthrown him' — and that was the essential difference. Though
he began to deal with abuses, and what he calls there the scandalous
life, and the evils and so on, yet he was on a deeper level at the same
time. He attacked the pope's doctrine, and he overthrew the entire
edifice. The volcanic man, this outstanding genius, was the man
who was thus led to initiate the Protestant Reformation. But, great
though he was, he could not have done it as a man, he could not have
done it alone.

The action of God

What do we see in this event? What do we see as we look at the whole
of the Protestant Reformation? There is only one thing to say: we see
the action of God. It is the only explanation. Luther, as I have told
you, was a great man, he was a true genius, but he is of all men, I
sometimes think, the one that is most comforting to the preacher. He
is not only comforting to preachers; he is a comfort, I am sure, to
many others who are here tonight. Genius, brilliant brain that he
was, he was subject to attacks of depression — he could be terribly
depressed. He was very human. Not only did he suffer from attacks
of depression, he was a great hypochondriac, particularly with

respect to his bowels. He talked a lot about that. That is why I mention it.

Not only that, if ever a man was attacked by the devil it was this man. We are told that the story of his throwing the ink-pot at the devil is not true — well, I don't know. But whether that is true or not, that he was attacked by the devil is beyond any question. He endured veritable onslaughts of Satan upon him. Moreover, he had to face staggering difficulties and problems. I say this again mainly for the comfort of my brethren in the ministry. In 1521 he had to spend a number of months in the Wartburg Castle to be saved from his enemies, and consequently was not in contact with the church and affairs at Wittenberg. After he got back to Wittenberg, after this incarceration, as it virtually was, in this place — when he got back to Wittenberg he found that all sorts and kinds of things had happened. Any man in the ministry knows what that kind of experience is. Church members are often like children. When the parents are away they tend to do certain things. The poor minister, when he comes back after a temporary absence, often finds the church in real trouble; all sorts of things have been happening in his absence. Poor Luther came back and he felt at first that the whole of the Reformation had been lost. He was cast down to the depths; but not for long. God would always raise him up. It is the only explanation of his amazing career. In spite of his natural depression and morbidity, in spite of this weakness with regard to ill-health and so on, and in spite of the devil, he was not down for long; he would rise up and he would cleanse the whole place again. He went on doing that throughout his extraordinary life.

So what I see above everything here is the action of God. Do you not see it? Look at the preparation for Luther and the Reformation — Wycliffe and Hus and other men; look at those mystics I have mentioned. They were all produced by God. It was a part of God's preparation for this mighty event that he knew was coming.

Then the Renaissance, the rediscovery of Greek culture, the work of Erasmus and others with the Greek New Testament and so on: it is part of God's preparation. Indeed there was even a political preparation. Many of the governors, princes and rulers in Germany were getting very restive about all the money that they had to be sending down to Rome constantly. They wanted to use it in their own way, but they were vassals of the pope; and so they were restive. There was political unrest.

Now some of the modern infidel historians think they can explain the whole of the Protestant Reformation in political terms. That, of course, is sheer nonsense. But it did come in, and God was behind it.

Then, and perhaps most important of all, there was the discovery of printing just at the right time. Oh, my friends, we are worshippers of a wonderful God! How perfect is his plan, how perfect is his timing! He does a thing there, and you feel that is only political, that is only economic; he does another thing here, and you say that this is only a matter of erudition or of culture. But no! They are all parts of a great plan. He sees it all, and he prepares parts and portions, and he had been doing this for over a century. Then the moment struck and he brought them all together; and he brought them all together in this astounding man, Martin Luther.

You do not get reformations through an Erasmus; it is through a Luther. This is about the only man I have ever read of in history who could have done it; any other man would have been crushed. Nothing could crush this man. God knew his man; he had made him, he had prepared him and he had filled him with his Spirit. It was he who had raised him up. So it did not matter what happened. No. Your dry-as-dust theologians and your scholars never lead to reformations. Incidentally, that is one of the things that is so obvious about this modern ecumenical movement. It is mainly a movement of professors and ecclesiastics. They lack this volcanic element, this living element, this experimental element, this experiential element, which is at the very heart and centre of the story of Martin Luther and the Protestant Reformation.

How do you explain him? How do you explain what he did? To me there is only one explanation and here it is. We read at the beginning of the third chapter of the Gospel according to Luke, 'In the fifteenth year of Tiberius Cæsar, Pontius Pilate being governor of Judæa', and so on,'The word of God came to John the son of Zacharias in the wilderness.' That is what happened in 1517, and just before: 'The word of God *came* to Martin Luther.' It is God from beginning to end. Listen to the way Luther himself puts it. He says, 'God led me on, like a horse whose eyes had been blindfolded that he may not see those who are rushing towards him.' That is all: 'God led me on.' He was like a horse who had been blindfolded so that he could not see the enemies that were coming to attack him with their chariots and their spears. 'I could not see, but God could, and he led me on. He did it; I but read and I but expounded and I but preached,' says Luther. 'It was the Word that did it; God led me on.' It is the only explanation; and that is our only comfort.

The lessons for today

Finally, let me apply what I have just been saying to our present state in just a few words. What does all this teach us? It is good, I say, to read history; it is good to study the lives of these men whom God has raised in the church from time to time. But we must do so not out of a mere antiquarian interest, not merely because of our historical curiosity, but in order that we may learn certain great spiritual lessons. What are the lessons, then, that we draw from Luther and the Reformation?

The first is this — the vital importance of the starting-point. What I mean is this: when you are confronted with a church in trouble, as the church is today, and we are concerned to know what we can do about it, there is nothing more important than your starting-point. Or if I may vary that, the lesson of Luther to me is the realization of the crucial importance of your first question. It is the first question you ask that matters. If your first question is wrong you will probably be wrong altogether. Or if I may put it in yet another form, the great lesson is this: the all-important distinction between the religious motive and ecclesiasticism.

Let me translate that into practical terms. What do we learn? First, what is the first question that we should ask at the present time? I answer: it is not, 'How can we have one territorial church?' That is not the first question. It was not Luther's first question. He had been brought up under that. That must never be the first question. Surely the whole tragedy today, and especially with regard to the ecumenical movement, is that people are asking the wrong first question. They start with the conditions as they are, and they say, 'How can we get one territorial church in each country, and then get them all to be in fellowship together in "one great world-church"?' It is the wrong question.

Or I can put that in another way. It is a wrong question to start with to ask, 'How can we have unity and fellowship?' Now unity is all-important. Our Lord has commanded it. But it is not the first question. You must not start with unity, you must not start with fellowship.

Thirdly, you must not start by asking, 'How can we find a formula that will satisfy men of diametrically opposed views?'

I am mentioning the very questions that are being asked at the present time. These are the questions of the ecumenically-minded people. They are seeking formulæ which will satisfy men whose views are diametrically opposed. Let me give you two illustrations of what I mean.

There has been considerable rejoicing in a certain section of the church in this country over the fact that they have now found a formula concerning the question of 'prayers for the dead'. Why are they so jubilant? They themselves supply the answer. They say that the formula they have at last evolved satisfies both the Anglo-Catholic and the evangelical. The same words. This is what is so marvellous! The Anglo-Catholic reads it and says, 'This is praying for the dead'; the evangelical looks at the same words and says, 'It is not praying for the dead at all,' but they are both equally happy to accept it. This is regarded as wonderful because it is a formula that holds the church together. Everybody can accept the formula, the magic formula, though they interpret it in diametrically opposed ways.

Or take another example, the question of the notorious 'service of reconciliation', as it is called, in connection with the Anglican/ Methodist proposals for the reunion of those two churches. Again this is the position: they have arrived at a formula. The Anglo-Catholic reads it and says, 'This means that this Methodist minister is being reordained.' The Methodist ministers — many of them, most of them probably — read it and say, 'This does not mean that we are being reordained.' Once more this is regarded as marvellous, because they are all agreed. They have got a marvellous formula; and though two groups are fundamentally opposed in their doctrine, it satisfies both sides and so they achieve 'unity'.

That is what happens when you start by asking, 'How can we find a formula that is going to bring us together and to hold us together?' And you are bound to ask that question if you start with the notion of a territorial church, if you start with unity and uniformity, in a sense, and fellowship, instead of with the true questions.

What, then, are the true questions? There is no difficulty in answering. Martin Luther answers. How did he start? How did he become the man he was? What led to the Protestant Reformation? Do you know the answer? Here is the first question, and here is the first question that the Christian church needs to ask today: *what is a Christian?* That is the first question. What is a Christian? Is he just a man who objects to atomic bombs and to war? Is he just a man who objects to apartheid? What is a Christian?

Luther, I feel, is thundering down the ages to us until this very night, and he is saying to us, 'Ask that question, "What is a Christian?" Do not start with organizations and institutions, do not start with territorial churches, or the idea of getting them all together, do not start with social and political questions; ask the great question which the Scriptures raise: "What is a Christian?"'

And the second — and, oh, how vital it was to Luther! *How does one become a Christian?* How does one find a gracious God? How does one get forgiveness of sins? Is it because I am christened as an infant? Is it because I am born in a particular country? What makes me a Christian? How do I become a Christian? Do I get pardon and forgiveness by paying for indulgences or by doing good works? How does one become a Christian and get this assurance of being reconciled to God? That is the question that led to the Protestant Reformation. It was this intense personal experience of salvation. And these are still the fundamental questions.

And they lead to the next: *what is a church?* Is she but an organization or institution, or is she the gathering of those who have had this experience of salvation and sins forgiven, and who know God, who are born again and have the Spirit witnessing within them? What is the church? Before you begin talking about amalgamations and unions let us ask the first question: what is a church?

I suggest to you that if we start with those questions we shall inevitably find ourselves following precisely the same path as was trodden by Martin Luther. It is inevitable.

Why? For these reasons: to a man who knows this experience, to a man who has his only authority in the Scriptures, there is no possible compromise with, first of all, the church of Rome — no possible compromise. The man who asks these questions and finds the scriptural answer finds, as Luther found, that it is impossible to come to any agreement with Rome. She teaches 'another gospel'. It is entirely different. There can be no compromise with sacerdotalism. There can be no compromise for the evangelical with those who say that a bishop is of the *'esse'* — the very essence — of the church. There is no compromise for the evangelical with a man who says that unless you have received episcopal ordination you are not truly ordained. It is impossible. There can be no accommodation between the evangelical and those who believe in the blasphemy of the 'mass'. There is no possible compromise for the evangelical with a belief in baptismal regeneration: it is impossible. Luther found it impossible as he went on studying and preparing his lectures on Romans and his sermons on the Psalms and Galatians, and so the break was inevitable.

But not only is compromise with such people impossible for the evangelical; it is equally impossible for him to be yoked together with others in the church who deny the very elements of the Christian faith, with men who seem to deny the very being of God and who convey the impression that the Lord Jesus Christ was a homosexual! There is no agreement between evangelicals and such teaching, for it is a question of light and darkness! The very desire to hold such groups together in one territorial church is surely a virtual denial of the Christian faith. It also raises the question of guilt by association. If you are content to function in the same church with such people — the two groups I have mentioned — you are virtually saying that though you think you are right, they also may be right, and this is a possible interpretation of Scripture. That, I assert, is a denial of the evangelical, the only true, faith. It is impossible.

But someone may object at this point and say, 'But are you not forgetting that Rome is changing? Are you not yourself falling back to the sixteenth century? Have you not been carried away by Luther? Are you forgetting that you are living in the twentieth century and that Rome is changing?'

All right, let us examine the change. The church of Rome today is not identical with the church in Luther's day. In what respects? Well, since then she has pronounced infallibly the doctrine of papal infallibility. That was done in 1870. What else? She has pronounced infallibly also the doctrine of the 'immaculate conception', and also the doctrine of the 'assumption of Mary'. Moreover there has been a terrible increase in Mariolatry. The only difference between the church of Rome then and now is this — that it is even worse now. Oh, yes, it is true to say that they have dealt with the question of the abuse of indulgences since Luther's day; but what they have also done is to degenerate in doctrine and to make it even worse than it was in his day. Let us not forget that. Then others say, 'What about their new attitude to the Bible?' Let us face it. Did you know that the new attitude to the Bible in the Roman church is mainly a higher-critical attitude, and that what is coming into the Roman church is modernism, liberalism, higher criticism — not evangelicalism? Do not be deluded, my friends! Those are the facts concerning the Roman Catholic Church.

'But wait,' says another, 'surely you ought to be concerned about these people in the church of Rome who are beginning to feel unhappy?' That is right; there are undoubtedly many in trouble. They say, 'Now surely you should be concerned about them and be anxious to help them.' I agree. We should be very concerned; we should be praying for them and for their conversion. But how are we to help them? Are we to help them by saying to them, 'You know, after all, there is not very much difference between us. We also have been moving, and we are coming much nearer together, and the step you have to take when you leave Rome and join one of our Protestant churches is a very small one'? Is that the way to help them? God forbid! If you want to help a troubled Roman Catholic show him the true doctrine, open the Scriptures to him, show him the error under which he has been brought up, show him how the things to which he has been trusting are denials of the gospel, even as Luther found in his day and generation.

And I can tell you this: if you take a stand on the Scriptures and on the truth, you will find that you are the very man of all men whom this troubled Roman Catholic will be most anxious to see. He will respect your honesty. He will say, 'This man knows where he is and what he believes. This is the man who can help me.' Not your com-promiser, who is prepared to give up most of what he stands for in order to help somebody else. No, no! This is true psychologically, and it has been true historically. There is a strange attraction in opposites, and if you really want to help these people, the way to do so is to be certain of what you believe. Do not apologize for it; expound it in love and with patience, and urge upon them the importance of giving it a wholehearted allegiance.

So I close with an appeal. The position round and about us is developing rapidly. The ecumenical movement is advancing day by day, and it is travelling in the direction of Rome. You need not take that from me. A great Methodist Old Testament scholar, Professor Norman Snaith, said that in print recently: 'It is heading towards

Rome.' Of course it is. But it is not only heading to Rome, it is heading also towards an amalgamation with the so-called world religions, and will undoubtedly end as a great World Congress of Faiths — anything in order to hold on to power and authority. Let us realize that.

Let us realize also that one territorial church in each country is only possible at the price of compromise of evangelical principles. The idea that evangelicals can infiltrate any established church — above all, the church of Rome — and reform it, and turn it into an evangelical body, is midsummer madness. No institution has ever been truly reformed. The Puritan movement and 1662 bear eloquent testimony to that fact. This is the verdict of history. Neutrality at a time like this is cowardice; it is temporizing, where it is not sheer ignorance of the facts.

What then are we as evangelicals to do in this situation? I reply by saying that we must heed a great injunction in Revelation 18:4: 'Come out of her, my people!' 'Come out of her, my people, that ye be not partakers of her sins, and that ye receive not of her plagues.' Come out of it! But come together also, come into fellowship with all like-minded Christian people. Come into an association such as this British Evangelical Council, that stands for the truth and against compromise, hesitation, neutrality and everything that but ministers to the success of the plans of Rome and the ecumenical movement. Come out; come in!

And then look back at old Martin Luther and say with him, 'Here I stand, I can do no other; so help me God!' and trust in him. What do numbers matter? What do sarcasm and scorn and derision matter? What does it matter though we be despised and laughed at? An ecumenical leader said the other day that 'Everybody believes in the ecumenical movement' — everybody! We are nobody, you see. Let them say it! This one man Luther was enabled by God to stand, as it were, against the whole church and against those centuries of tradition. And you and I will be enabled to do the same. Let us use his words, and believe them:

God's Word, for all their craft and force,
One moment will not linger,
But, spite of hell, shall have its course;
'Tis written by his finger.

And though they take our life,
Goods, honour, children, wife,
Yet is their profit small;
These things shall vanish all:
The city of God remaineth.

Do you belong to her — 'Zion, city of our God?' When everything else has gone, 'The city of God remaineth.'

God grant that all of us may know of a surety that we are members and citizens of that city.

3.
What is the church?

This address was given on 13 November 1968 at Toxteth Tabernacle, Liverpool, where the BEC was holding its second major conference. It complemented the subject which the Rev. Herbert M. Carson had dealt with the previous evening, which was, 'What is a Christian?' Those two questions, 'What is a Christian?' and 'What is a church?' were chosen for the conference programme because the Doctor had shown in his address on Luther how basic they were and how urgently they needed to be treated.

Both addresses were printed separately in booklet form. What is the Church? *appeared in July 1969.*

My subject follows naturally, logically from the subject, 'What is a Christian?' The two subjects are intimately related. You cannot separate these two things; they belong, and must inevitably go, together. The one big difference is that this is the more difficult of the two, and that for this reason. There is very little disagreement amongst evangelical people as to 'What is a Christian?' but unfortunately you cannot say the same thing about the views of evangelical people with regard to the question of 'What is the church?' Unfortunately there is disagreement here, as I am going to try to show you, and that is why my task is a difficult one.

The importance of the question

Why should we consider these questions? As we saw in the Luther commemoration, any consideration of the Reformation makes this

inevitable. But that is not all. Why is it our duty to consider this?
There are many answers to that question. I am going to deal with
them as briefly as I can.

The first is the very fact and existence of what is called the
ecumenical movement. The rapidity with which things are happening, whether we like them or not, is quite alarming. The fact is that
movements are afoot to unite churches, and eventually to unite all
the churches, and to have one great territorial church in this country,
and one great worldwide church. The thing is happening rapidly.
And while we are dallying and considering and talking, events are
taking place, and unless we act — and act quickly — we shall find
ourselves in a position in which we have very little that we can really
do.

That is one reason. But another and more important one is this:
I want to suggest to you that it is this trouble with regard to the true
understanding of the nature of the church that is one of the greatest
hindrances to evangelism. Now what we are constantly being told
is this, that we should work together, and evangelize together in
particular, and not be bothered about these discussions about the
nature of the church and our different views. But this is a very false
argument, it seems to me. How can you evangelize truly unless you
are agreed about the evangel? It seems to me to be a sheer
impossibility. 'If the trumpet yield an uncertain sound, who shall
prepare him for the battle?' What is the gospel? I have often said that
I am not surprised that the majority of people in this country today
are outside the Christian church. As they listen to the talks on the
television and the wireless, and read in the newspapers these
contradictory statements that are made in the name of the Christian
church with regard to the gospel of Jesus Christ, how can they listen
truly? The confusion in which they are to be found is a confusion
that is caused by the church herself and her discordant and contradictory voices. So I suggest that failure to be clear about the doctrine
of the church is one of the greatest hindrances to true evangelism at
this present time.

It is likewise the cause of some of the methods that have been
used in evangelism during this present century. Some things that are
being done with the best intentions in the world, it seems to me,
could never have been done had men and women realized the true
nature of the Christian church.

In the same way, the trouble about this doctrine is surely the greatest hindrance to revival. Can the Holy Spirit honour anything save the truth? Can we expect the Spirit to come in power upon a people that know not the truth, and sometimes even deny it and are antagonistic to it? The thing is patently impossible. So if we want revival we must start by considering this doctrine of the nature of the Christian church.

Another reason for considering it is this: that it is, alas, the greatest cause of division amongst evangelicals in this country at the present time. Now we are not concerned with one another's motives. We know that we are all equally honest and equally sincere. It is not a question of persons; it is a question of attitudes and points of view. But there is no doubt that this is the major cause of division amongst evangelical people in this country today.

Another reason for considering it is this: that it has been the sheer failure to consider the doctrine of the church that has led, during the past ninety years in particular, to the terrible confusion that is to be found amongst us at the present time. Movements come into being, men set themselves up and form their own organization, men enter pulpits without any church ever considering whether they have been called or not, and so on. The state of our churches is one of confusion, and it is ultimately due to the fact that we have not troubled to consider the New Testament doctrine concerning the nature of the church. In our zeal and anxiety to do good and to evangelize, we have rushed into action without considering how these things should be truly done.

But, of course, the ultimate and greatest reason for considering this doctrine is the fact that it is given such great prominence in the New Testament teaching. Have you ever realized this? Practically every single New Testament epistle really deals with this doctrine of the question of the nature of the Christian church.

Now this, of course, is something that is really quite inevitable; for when we are saved we are not merely saved as individuals, we are not meant to be isolated units; immediately we are added to the church. You get that in the book of Acts; you get it everywhere. 'No man is an island.' If that is true in general it is particularly true of the Christian — immediately, he becomes part of a body. This is God's own ordained plan and method. So the New Testament obviously deals with this, and deals with it very exhaustively. Not only that,

I think I could demonstrate very simply that the trouble that arose
in various ways even in the early church in the first century was
nearly always due to a defective understanding of the doctrine of the
nature of the church.

Let me give you one illustration. Take that great first epistle of
Paul to the Corinthians. It is a long epistle of some sixteen chapters;
and he wrote it because he had to, in a sense. A number of problems
had arisen in the church at Corinth, and in every single case the
apostle points out to them that these troubles had arisen simply
because they were not clear in their minds as to the nature of the
Christian church.

Look at that division into sects: 'I am of Paul; I am of Apollos;
I am of Cephas; I am of Christ.' Paul is amazed at them, and he says,
'Is Christ divided?' You only get sects like this arising in a church
over persons when people are not clear with regard to the doctrine
of the whole nature of the church.

Then he goes on to deal in chapter 5, you remember — having
dealt with that first question in the first four chapters — with the case
of that incestuous person in the church, and he deals with it in
exactly the same way. He does not merely deal with the problem of
incest, as we tend to do at the present time, and talk about the details
of the particular thing; he immediately puts it into the context of the
church. He says, 'Know ye not that a little leaven leaveneth the
whole lump?' He says, 'If you understood the character of the
church you would never tolerate this.'

In the sixth chapter, when he deals with the question of their
going to law in public courts with one another over their disputes,
he deals with it in exactly the same way. He says, 'Isn't there
somebody in the church? Why don't you appoint the most insignificant person in the church, and set him up as judge? Do you not know
that you are going to judge angels?' Their trouble was due to the fact
that they had not understood this doctrine of the church.

In the same way he deals with marriage and the question of
children. In the same way he deals with the question of 'the weaker
brother'. There were men in the church who were troubled about
eating meats that had been offered to idols and so on, and this was
causing great confusion in the church. The stronger, more enlightened members were despising the weaker members in the matter of
understanding, and they were dividing the church. He deals with
that in exactly the same terms.

And on he goes. You remember how he deals with the question of coming to the communion table and eating the bread and drinking the wine. One loaf! That is the church. And then, of course, when you come to the great vexed question of the spiritual gifts in chapters 12, 13 and 14, the matter is dealt with entirely in terms of the doctrine of the church. They would never have been quarrelling about tongues and prophecies and miracles, and all these various other matters, and dividing over these things, if they had only understood the doctrine of the nature of the church. You see, if you are not clear about this you will certainly get into trouble in theory and in practice. So the way to deal with these matters, and indeed the way to avoid getting troubles and problems and difficulties, is to start by being clear with regard to the doctrine of the nature of the church.

Those, then, are the reasons why we must do this, and there are many others. Obviously in one address no man can deal with a subject like this fully and exhaustively. Learned tomes, many volumes, have been written on this subject. I am simply going to pick out what I regard as being most important, and particularly what is most relevant to our position at this present moment. I am not going to deal with the question of the visible and the invisible church; I am not going to deal with questions of church government and polity, and many other aspects of this whole problem of the doctrine of the nature of the church. I am not going to deal with it in a formal or academic manner. I am simply going to try to give you a picture. For it is my view that the trouble with all of us, not only people who are not evangelical, not only Roman Catholic, but even those of us who are evangelical, I suggest our main trouble is that we are not clear on this whole question of the nature of the church.

The essence of the doctrine

What is the essence of this doctrine? Let me try to summarize the teaching of the New Testament concerning this question. How do we deal with it? Well, we must not deal with it by just starting from where we are. That, I believe, is the greatest fallacy of all. The danger is to start with it as it is. This is a very good procedure when you are examining many problems. The medical man obviously has got to examine the patient in front of him, and it is right in many other matters. But when you come to this question of the church I believe this is a real danger; and this is what has generally been done. You start with the church as she is, and then you begin to consider how you can modify at this point and that point, where you can introduce an improvement, and so on. Now if you do that the danger is that you are leaving the basic question entirely unconsidered. So we must not just start from where we are, and then try to find some magical formula to bring us together or to smooth over difficulties. That is the road, it seems to me, to disaster. That is the fallacy, surely, of the ecumenical movement. So we do not start where we are.

I suggest also that it is not always wise to start even with history, for even history can be misleading. Our fathers were great and glorious men; we are hardly worthy to mention the names of the great ones. But even they were not infallible. They were creatures of their age, and they were often influenced, as we are, by their circumstances and conditions of the moment. So I think that we must avoid even that; because if we do not, we shall probably end by defending a particular tradition in which we happen to believe and in which, perhaps, we have been brought up. I suggest that the thing to do, the only honest thing to do ultimately, is to go back to the New Testament itself.

Now this is particularly important today, for we are in an age when everything is being examined anew and afresh. You get all the major denominations saying they are prepared to throw everything into the melting-pot. Very well, let us do so. Let us go back and try to discover from the New Testament itself what exactly is the nature of the church. Let us go back to the book of the Acts of the Apostles. Let us go back to the epistles. Do not misunderstand me: I am not dismissing history. All I am saying is, do not start with it; go back to the origins. Then, if you like, take your history and check your understanding of the teaching of Acts and the epistles by what men in history, and in their concrete situations, have thought and how they have interpreted the Scripture, and what they have done. We can learn from history, but we must not become slaves to history. The Scriptures, plus the advantage of being able to use the thoughts of those who have gone before us, should be our rule.

What, then, do we find? What is the church? What is a church? The first answer to the question is this: it is patently *a gathering of people*. That is what you get — is it not? — in the book of the Acts of the Apostles, a gathering of people — 120 people in an upper room; 3,000 people added to them; another 2,000 added to those, and on and on it goes. So you are looking at a gathering of people such as this one; a number of people have come together. This is basic in our definition as to what a church is. It is essentially, first and foremost, a gathering of people.

Well, somebody may say, 'Why are you putting all that emphasis upon what is so obvious?' I can answer that quite simply. I am doing this because I am compelled to do so, for there is a very prominent and well-known teaching at the present time which seems to regard a church not as a gathering or collection of people but as a confession of faith, or something written on paper. Now this is a very common argument amongst certain evangelical people who would not agree with many of us who are here tonight. Their argument for staying in their denominations is, 'As long as they do not change the confession of faith we are staying in. Of course,' they say, 'if they were to change the confession of faith we would go out at once.' Now I say that what is implicit in that is that a church ultimately is a confession of faith; it is a document; it is something that is written on paper. This, I believe, is the most important matter for our consideration, because it is just here that this terrible confusion has come in. This has always been an important matter, but it is, as I am saying, especially important at the present time.

Why is this so important? Why must we avoid this danger of forgetting that it is people, living people, that constitute a church, and not a number of propositions on paper? Well, there are many answers to this again. We must avoid that because that has always been the greatest cause of denominationalism. You are familiar with denominationalism, are you not? You know the sort of person who does not come and say to you, 'I am a Christian,' but says 'I am a Methodist,' or 'I am a Congregationalist.' I used to meet a great deal of this when I was minister at Westminster Chapel. A man would come in and say to me, 'I am a Methodist.' I knew all about him at once. Another would say, 'I am a Congregationalist.' All right, I knew exactly.

What causes this? This is generally the result of being ignorant of the real origin of the denomination, but just fighting for it because they had been brought up in it, or because it was 'their' denomination. This artificial thing was the thing that was gripping them, and they were fighting merely for a tradition.

That is one danger, but there is a much more serious one. This tendency to regard a confession of faith, whatever it be — whether the Thirty-Nine Articles or the Westminster Confession, it does not matter at all — all this can really be a lie; and I suggest that it is a lie, speaking generally, at the present time, and for this reason. Most people who are in these various churches at the present moment generally do not believe the confession of faith of the denomination to which they belong. I could illustrate that in all the denominations. But they remain in it, and it is a living lie. You have churches today in which people at the present time — preachers in pulpits and people in pews — not only do not believe the confessions of the founders of these bodies, but are active and bitter opponents of them. Yet the name goes on; and this is where to regard a church as a matter of a confession on paper really does become a lie. I would make bold to say this: what matters is not what fathers may have said in the sixteenth or the seventeenth century — what matters is, what do the people in that denomination believe today? That is the relevant and the vital question. To ignore that leads to utter confusion.

Then another reason is failure to realize that that has always been a high road to dead orthodoxy. Even when men believe the confession of faith it is no guarantee that they are Christians. You can get people who are perfectly orthodox and yet completely dead. You can get a dead orthodoxy. So if you put this confession first, this paper declaration first, and tend to judge your church and to regard what you call a church in terms of that, you may be covering a dead orthodoxy, where people may have the right belief but deny it in their lives, or where they have no experience of it and find it to be of no value to them in their hour of need.

Therefore I say that I must emphasize first that, whatever else the church is, she is a collection of people; you are looking at a body of people. That was what attracted the crowd on the Day of Pentecost. There were a number of people gathered together; that was the phenomenon — people. Not paper declarations, but people. So we have got to start with this.

This is unusually important in our day; because the ultimate answer to these friends who say that they are going to stay in their denominations until the confession of faith is changed is simply this, that the modern strategy is one which has already said, 'We are not going to change these; we will accept them all.' What they are really saying is, 'We will put them into the museum.' This is the new strategy. They are not going to change the Thirty-Nine Articles. What are they going to do? They say, 'Yes, we accept them all, but this is what we believe now.' One of the ecclesiastical authorities in defending this attitude said, 'We have got to do this in order to get on with the business.' So if you are going to wait until they change the confession you will find you will be there until you are dead; they are not going to change them. The modern subtle argument is, 'Let us take in everything, let us include everything. Let us pay lip service to everything, and then preach what we really believe.' So there is nothing which is more dangerous than to forget that a church is a collection of living people, persons, and not merely ancient declarations.

The uniqueness of the church

What, then, are these people? You are looking at a church; you are looking at a gathering, a collection of people. What are these people? There are many societies in the world; there are many gatherings and groupings. What is it that differentiates the church as a gathering, a collection of people, from every other kind of gathering? The answer is that there is a uniqueness about the church. There is something about the church that you never find anywhere else. What is it that constitutes the uniqueness? Let me mention some of these things.

The first is that it is a collection of people who have been separated from the world. They are living in the world like everybody else; they are human beings like everybody else: well, what is it that makes them special and unique? It is this: they have been separated from the life of the world. To use the glorious language of Paul in Colossians 1:13, they have been 'translated from the kingdom of darkness, into the kingdom of God's dear Son'. Or as Peter puts it equally gloriously, 'Ye are a chosen generation, a royal priesthood, an holy nation, a peculiar people; that ye should show forth the praises of him who hath called you out of darkness into his marvellous light: who were not a people, but are now the people of God: who had not obtained mercy, but now have obtained mercy' (1 Peter 2:9-10). This is it! It is this 'but now ... '. 'You were ...; you are ... '. What is this? Well, Peter tells us. 'Dearly beloved,' he says, 'I beseech you as strangers and pilgrims... ' This is the peculiar thing about these people: they are in the world, but they no longer belong to it; they are 'strangers and pilgrims'. This is the thing that has happened to them: they have been 'separated'.

The New Testament is full of these expressions. 'Ye are no longer of the night,' says Paul elsewhere, 'but children of the day.' What a separation—darkness and light! Night and day! The world, and God and heaven! 'Our citizenship is in heaven.' That is where we belong. We are still citizens of Liverpool or London; we are still citizens of Great Britain. But I belong to heaven. I am a stranger here. 'Strangers and pilgrims.' They have been separated; this is the first thing that is emphasized everywhere in the New Testament.

I want to elaborate this for a moment. You see, these people have been separated even from the state. They belong to it still in an external political sense, and yet their true citizenship is not there; it is elsewhere: it is in heaven. So the whole notion of a state-church is a complete contradiction of the basic statement of the New Testament about the nature of the church. It has nothing to do with the state, though its members still function as citizens in the state. I will go further: it is even a separation from nationality — and that is not an easy thing for some of us to say!

This conference, if it has done nothing else, has been a living illustration of the point I am making. Have those of you who have been here been observing it? If you had only been here yesterday you would have thought that the Christian church was exclusively Irish! If you had only been here today you might well have come to the conclusion that it was exclusively Welsh! But I was grateful for the extra session pushed in this afternoon when some Englishmen spoke!

I say that just to illustrate this point that, though we still belong to the nation in which we were born — and we are not meant to crucify that — nevertheless we are separated from it. Whatever I may feel as a Welshman, I put a Christian brother before a fellow Welshman. 'There is no longer Jew nor Gentile, Barbarian or Scythian, bond nor free' — black nor white, pink nor yellow. All these distinctions are superseded in the church. Though we remain in the flesh and we do not belittle these things, these are no longer the controlling matters in our thoughts. 'Henceforth', says Paul in 2 Corinthians 5, 'henceforth know I no man after the flesh'; and he had been a very nationalistic Jew. 'Henceforth know I no man after the flesh.' We are even separated from that.

We are separated also in this sense from all the orders of society. The man of the world recognizes certain orders of society; he at one time did it more than he does now: the squire, the lord, the great men in the district, and the various gradations down until you came to the underling. But there is no room for that in the New Testament. A man is not called to read the Scriptures in the New Testament because he is 'the lord of the manor'. That is done away with. James tells us not to give a front seat to a man because he has got a gold ring on. These distinctions do not apply here. These are all put on one side. We have been separated from all this. We are thinking in a new way. This is a new society, and you have to put all such considerations once and for ever out of your mind. There is no monarchical principle here, there is no aristocratic principle here. All are one in Christ Jesus, and all are saved by the same faith, and all are equally the children of God. So you are separated from all these things.

But I have got to go even further than that. These people who constitute the church may even have to be separated from their families and their nearest and dearest. 'Think not that I am come to send peace on earth,' says our Lord. 'I came not to send peace, but a sword.' Listen to what he says! How we tend to forget these words: 'I am come to set a man at variance against his father, and the daughter against her mother, and the daughter in law against her mother in law' (Matthew 10:34). Our Lord says the same thing again, you remember, in Luke 14. He says, 'If a man comes after me and does not hate' — these are his words, they are not mine — 'if he hate not his father, and mother, and wife, and children, and brethren, and sisters, yea, and his own life, he cannot be my disciple.' The church is a very unique gathering of people. All the old associations have been broken; all the old thinking has been put on one side. Here is a new body, here is a new gathering, and it is unique in that we have separated from all this.

Now this is the thing that passes my comprehension at the present time — that whereas the New Testament tells us that in order to belong to the church we may have to even be 'separated' from father, or mother, or husband, or wife, or even brothers or sisters, there are evangelicals who still prefer to be in communion with, and in fellowship with, infidels and deniers of the gospel rather than separate and align themselves exclusively with brother evangelicals. We are even to separate from father and mother in this matter, and yet that is the attitude of so many at this present hour.

Brethren, is it not time we began to consider the New Testament teaching about the doctrine of the church? It involves a separation; it is new; it is unique; there is nothing like it in the universe, and never has been.

The unity of the church

Let me hurry to the second characteristic, which is unity. I say unity, not fellowship. I put this again very prominently; I put it in the second position. I put it before doctrine, you notice. Why? Because all the New Testament pictures of the church emphasize it. What are they? What is the church? She is compared to a body; she is compared to a bride; she is compared to a family; she is compared to a building; she is compared to a commonwealth. And all the explicit statements emphasize this same thing: 'They continued steadfastly.' They were together considering the apostles' doctrine, and so on.

This unity is emphasized right through the whole of the New Testament. We are told by our Lord himself that it is to be a visible unity. It is to be something that the world can see 'in order that the world may know', he says, 'that thou hast sent me', and that he is in us and that we are in him. The world is to 'see' this; the church is to manifest and demonstrate a visible unity. In other words, a church is not a place where men come together in order to seek for truth, or to have a debate as to what is truth, or where they may have what is called now a 'dialogue' in order that they may be able to smooth over their difficulties. It is not a place of argument and discussion in order that you may 'arrive' at something. No, no! The word that is used about people who become Christians and church members in the New Testament is this: 'They were *added* to the church.' Why were they added to the church? The answer is, because of something that had already happened to them. A church is not a forum for discussion. You can only become a member of a church in the New Testament after the discussion is over. It is only 'because' certain things had happened to them that they were added to the church.

There is a very significant statement in the Old Testament that throws light on this. You get the church in the Old Testament in pictures. Do you remember that very interesting bit of instruction given in connection with the erection of the temple? We are told that the stones that were to be put into the walls of the temple were to be chiselled into shape before they were brought to the temple, so that there should be no sound of an axe or of a hammer as the temple was being built. The stones were quarried and then they were chiselled, and so on, into shape far away from the temple. After they had been prepared they were then brought into the temple precincts and there they were built up in silence. That is the church! Not an official of one cathedral criticizing the officials of another cathedral, and so creating a public scandal, and causing confusion to the man in the street as to what the Christian church really is. Not brawling and argument and disruption. Not one man getting up and saying one thing, another getting up in the same pulpit and contradicting it next Sunday. My friends, that is not the church; that is confusion and Babel. There was to be no sound as the building went up; it was to be erected in silence. Why? Well, because the work had already been done. And that is what you find everywhere in the New Testament about the church.

Who were the people who were added to the church? They were always people, as was said last night, who had passed through, and had shared, a common experience. What are these experiences? Here they are.

They had known conviction of sin. If you have not known conviction of sin you are not a Christian, and you are not really a member of the church. These people had undergone conviction of sin; they had cried out saying, 'Men and brethren, what shall we do?' Have you known it? I am not asking whether you are a Methodist or Congregationalist, or a member of an FIEC church or anything else. I am asking, have you known conviction of sin?

They had also repented; they had also confessed their sin; they had also expressed a desire to turn from it, and had turned from it.

But above and beyond everything else, *they had been 'born again'.* 'Verily, verily, I say unto you, except a man be born again, he cannot see the kingdom of God' — leave alone enter it. It is impossible. This is something that is vital; but we have been tending to forget this. These men had passed through this same experience; they had got new life. 'The natural man receiveth not the things of the Spirit of God: for they are foolishness unto him: neither can he know them, because they are spiritually discerned.' The only man who is a member of the church is a man who has got new life: he is 'born anew', 'born again', 'born of the Spirit'. He is regenerated; he has got a new mind, a new understanding; he has 'the mind of Christ'. 'He that is spiritual judgeth all things, yet he himself is judged of no man.' He is a strange man; he has become an enigma to his friends. They say of him, 'Why will you not come with us as you used to? What has happened to you?' And if this sort of thing is not true of us we are not Christian. He is a changed man; he is a new man; he is a man who is born anew, born of the Spirit; he is a partaker of the divine nature. Christ is in him. The Spirit is in him. In other words, these people are unique because they are sharing a common life, and this is the most vital thing of all. Peter says that as Christians, members of churches, we are 'lively' or 'living stones'.

In other words, you see, this question of life, and this emphasis upon the church as a body, reminds us that the unity that is characteristic of the church is an organic unity; it is a vital unity. Look at the obvious illustration. What is a body? Is it a mere collection of fingers and hands and arms and forearms stuck together, anyhow, loosely? Of course it is not. It is organic, it is one, it is vital.

This is the great principle emphasized everywhere in the New Testament. 'Know ye not'', says Paul, 'that ye are the temple of God?' 'Know ye not that ye are a habitation of God through the Spirit?' This is the church. Not an institution, not a mere gathering of people as such, but these special people who, because they have all undergone this same experience of regeneration, share the same life; it is in them. As the members of a family have the same blood, and this essential community resulting from that, so have these people. They are born from above, born of the Spirit, born of God, children of God. These are the terms; and we must never fail to put this in the first position because, thank God, a Christian primarily is not even a man who believes the right things: he is 'a new man in Christ Jesus'; he is 'a new creation'; he is one who is 'born of the Spirit' and is a 'partaker of the divine nature'.

This has got to come first because it is the only way to avoid a dead orthodoxy. You and I are living in this evil hour in the history of the Christian church very largely because of what became true of our grandfathers. I am old enough to remember some of them. They held on to their orthodoxy, but many of them had lost the life. They had 'a form of godliness but they denied the power thereof'. The only way you can safeguard yourself from a dead orthodoxy is to put life before even orthodoxy. It is a life. Not only that, you find in the New Testament everywhere that all the appeals for unity are based upon this. The argument is, 'Can you treat your brother like that?' When Paul deals with this question of meats offered to idols, and drinking various things, that is his argument. He says, 'Do you not know that this weak man is your brother for whom Christ died? Can you offend him?' You have no argument ultimately and you cannot deal with your ethical problems except in that way. You have no sanction to apply unless you believe this doctrine of the unity in terms of 'life'. It is not merely the rightness or the wrongness of the thing; Paul says, 'conscience not thine own, but of the other also'. This may be right for you, but if it is a hindrance to your weaker brother you must not do it.

In other words, it is not a mere bit of argumentation about ethics; it is this great argument of the unity of the body, that we are all in the same family; and therefore he appeals in terms of this. And as you know, in the great appeal of 1 Corinthians 13, Paul says you may have all knowledge, you may understand all mysteries, you may speak with tongues of men and angels, but if you are lacking in love, in this true charity, in this true relationship to your brother, it is no use to you; you are 'sounding brass, tinkling cymbal'. It is useless. 'Though you give your body to be burned,' it is of no value. This is the primary thing that must always be emphasized.

Ultimately, and lastly under this heading, this is what makes schism such a terrible sin. It is not merely that you disagree with others: it is that you are dividing Christ; you are dividing a body; you are dividing a family. And so the apostle brings out his mighty powers of ridicule in 1 Corinthians 12. He says, 'What would you think of a hand that said to a foot, "I have no need of you", or any eye that said to a hand, "I have no need of you"?' You would say that that is lunacy. You see, he ridicules it because of this great argument. He says, 'You are dividing the body.' It does not matter what gift you have; it does not matter how humble, nor significant. To one he says, 'Do not be envious of a man with a great gift,' and to the man with a great gift he says, 'Do not despise the man with a little gift. What you both ought to be boasting about is this, that you are in the body.' What a wonderful thing it is to be a little finger in such a body, or even a 'less comely part' — even that! You see, it is only in terms of this doctrine that he is able to show the terrible character of the sin of schism. For brethren who are agreed about the essentials of the gospel, and who are sharing the same life, to be divided by history, tradition, or any consideration, is the sin of schism, and it is a terrible sin.

The life of the church

But let us just take another glance at these people, and just ask a few questions as to how this life, this wonderful unity, this wonderful life, shows itself. The first way in which it always shows itself is this: that *they have a love of the same doctrine* always. 'They continued steadfastly in the apostles' doctrine' — doctrine before fellowship, doctrine before breaking of bread, doctrine before prayer. It is the reverse today, is it not? Fellowship is the great thing. 'Let us all get together, let us all pray together.' No, no! Doctrine first. Why? Well, this is inevitable. A man who has got something of the life of God in his soul is always a man who desires to know the teaching and doctrine. Peter uses this as a comparison: 'As newborn babes, desire the sincere milk of the word, that ye may grow thereby.' How do you know that that little child that has just been born is a live child and not a dead birth? The answer is, the live child makes for the milk. Every young animal does the same; it makes for the food. Its nature demands it, cries out for it. And the man who is born again is a man who wants teaching.

I want to ask you some plain questions — I am addressing evangelical people. Do you enjoy doctrine? Do you enjoy sermons on doctrine? Are you interested in teaching? I sometimes hear from my brethren that they visit churches where a limit is put on the length of their sermon, and indeed on the content of their sermon. The people say they cannot follow doctrine; they are bored by doctrine. They want entertainment; they want more singing; they want more 'happiness', they say, and they do not want doctrine.

Now I am free to admit that a man may preach doctrine in such a dull manner that it really is very boring. I am making no defence of that. But I am here to say this: that unless you have got a desire within you to know more of this precious blessed truth, you cannot be a child of God. It is impossible. This child craves for it, as the babe always makes for the milk.

How vitally important this is for us in every department of our lives! Do you not see the dangers? Look at the false teachings round about us. How can I be safe with regard to these unless I have got an objective standard? Take all this emphasis upon experience. People say, 'I don't care what you believe as long as you have had an experience, or your life has been changed, or you are a good and a kind man, and so on.' But my dear friend, the cults can talk like that, and they do talk like that. How do you know that you are right, and that the man who is selling you those books at your front door is not right? How do you prove it? It is no use saying, 'Well, I have had an experience.' He says he has had one. It is no use saying, 'I am zealous in my church.' He is. He gives up watching football on Saturday afternoons to go round from house to house to sell his books. He is very zealous, probably more than you are. How do you tell whether a man is right or wrong? You cannot in terms of zeal and enthusiasm or experience. There is only one ultimate test — objective truth. The teaching! The doctrine! It is not what a man thinks or believes, but what is this deposit that has come down? We are founded on 'the foundation of the apostles and prophets'. Here is the only foundation, and if we depart from this we have gone hopelessly and helplessly astray.

And if you want to help others, how can you unless you know the teaching and the doctrine? What is the use of going to a friend and saying, 'I have undergone a great change. I am very happy now. You remember how miserable I used to be; I am very happy now,' and this and that. 'Well,' they say, 'yes, you know, a Christian Scientist said the same thing to me yesterday. What is the difference?' What do you say to them? Oh, says the apostle Peter, 'Be ready at all times to give a reason for the hope that is in you.' You have got to be able to give them an understanding. You have got to be able to tell them. You have got to give them an explanation. If you want to help others you must know your doctrine, you must understand the teaching. So this is the thing that is put first.

And then you come to *fellowship*; but you cannot have fellowship unless you are agreed. 'Can two walk together except they be agreed?' How can you ever have real fellowship with a man when you know that he does not believe in the deity of Christ and in his atoning sacrifice? It is impossible. Fellowship is based upon truth.

'Breaking of bread.' What are we commemorating in our communion service? Is it the death of a pacifist? Is it a tragedy that once took place? Or is it, as we believe, the most glorious thing that has

ever happened? 'When I survey the *wondrous* cross…!' How can I come to the table with a man who ridicules the blood of Christ and pours scorn on the preaching about the blood? 'Grovelling in blood,' they say. The blasphemies that they speak against the blood, the precious blood of Christ, the Lamb of God! You cannot partake truly at the table with a man who holds such views. Doctrine is essential to fellowship and breaking of bread.

And to *prayer*. They say, 'We can all pray together. We do not agree perhaps, but we can always pray together.' But you cannot. What is prayer? How do you get access to God? One man says that all you need do is to sit on a comfortable chair and relax and start listening to God. Is that it? Another man says anybody can pray whenever he likes; God is always ready to listen. Is that right? Paul says, 'By him, by Christ crucified, we both have access by the one Spirit unto the Father.'

My friends, there is only one way to enter into the holiest of all; there is only one way to pray: it is 'by the blood of Jesus'. There is no acceptance with God except by the blood of Jesus. Unless you know that he is the one and only mediator between God and men there is no value in your prayer. God, in his love and grace, may answer you in spite of that, but you have not been praying. You cannot pray except in the way that is indicated and taught in the New Testament itself.

There is still one thing that I want to emphasize, in a sense above everything. I am looking at the New Testament church — we are looking at it together — and there we see them, 'continuing stead-fastly in the apostles' doctrine and fellowship, and in breaking of bread, and in prayer'. Yes, but we are told another thing about them. What is that? That they were *'filled with gladness'*. 'With gladness and singleness of heart they did eat their meat from house to house.' They were a very happy people. What is the matter today? Why are our churches empty? I can tell you. It is simply because you and I are such miserable people. That is what the man in the street says about us. He says, 'I am not going to join that miserable lot.' He says he has got happiness and joy, that he has got life. He says, 'Look at those miserable people, slinking into their morning services on Sunday, sitting as far back as they can, hoping it will soon come to an end.' He says, 'That is Christianity, that is your church!' My friends, you and I are responsible for the fact that the masses of people are outside the church. We give the impression far too often that to be a Christian is to be miserable, whereas the thing that characterized these New Testament people was 'gladness', 'joy'. They were the happiest people in the universe. These were people who could sing even in the mouths of the lions in the arena; they could sing in a prison at midnight. Listen to Paul and Silas singing, even with the stripes and the wounds and the agony, and the feet fast in the stocks: 'praying and singing praises unto God', in the darkness of midnight hour. Gladness and joy! Christian people, whether we are evangelical or not, we are useless until we manifest this radiant joy, and give our neighbours the impression that the only way to true and lasting joy and happiness is to become the children of God.

The other thing we are told about them is that they were *'praising God'*. Where has the praising gone in our churches? Thanking him for Christ, thanking him for what he had done for them, thanking God for what they were, thanking God for what they were yet to be —these are the things that bound these people together, these were their characteristics. There they were, day by day, meeting together in the temple and from house to house. And what were they doing? Oh, they were studying, they were listening and they were praising God and thanking *him;* they were singing psalms and hymns and spiritual songs. They were filled with ecstasy and the world was amazed.

With a world on fire, and hell let loose, with venereal disease having assumed epidemic proportions again in this country — not to talk about LSD and the other drugs — is this a time when the church should be arguing about episcopal ordination and vestments and niceties of terminology in liturgies? God have mercy upon us! What the world is waiting for is for a people who have been emancipated, released, set free, washed, cleansed, justified, renewed, made more than conquerors through him that has loved us. This is the church! This is the sort of people you should find in the church.

They also have *a great concern for the glory of God.* They are ready to die for this if necessary .They have got a concern for the glory of Christ and the Holy Ghost. They will give up everything for him. They say that to gain the whole world and to lose him is useless. But they have got *a great concern for others* also. They are troubled about their relatives who are outside; they are troubled about the poor man who is a slave to drink or to drugs or to anything else; they are sorry for him. They know. They have been there. They have been

delivered; they want him to be delivered. They have a heart of
compassion; they are like their Lord. He saw mankind 'as sheep
without a shepherd', and they see mankind as sheep without a shepherd, and they are anxious to tell others about this. And they did so,
and they have always done so in all times of real awakening. They
preached, they taught and they were filled with a power from God
through the Spirit to enable them to do this.

Spiritual power

It is with this I want to close. The New Testament church was a
pneumatic church. She was a church vibrating with life and with
power. They all took part. It was not a case of one man doing all the
talking, and all the praying, and all of everything else, and the others
just sitting and listening. They were all taking part. There were
differing gifts, but they all had some gift, and together they exercised this variety of gifts. But the thing that is so obvious about them
was their *liveliness*. 'Living stones,' says Peter. There was a life, an
energy, flowing through their very arteries, their spiritual arteries.
They were filled with this pneumatic power and all who met them
were always amazed at them: who are these people? That is why
they turned the world upside-down. There was this energy, this
ability, this joy, this happiness, this radiance: this was the thing that
changed the ancient world. And it was true of all of them: lively!
    We must examine ourselves in the light of this. The preaching
was lively. Some of us are terribly dull. A dull preacher is a
contradiction in terms. Lively preachers and lively listeners — that
is the New Testament church! And lively in prayer. The leaders did
not have to persuade them to take part in prayer; the difficulty was
to stop them all praying together at the same time. You see, this was
the problem — the problem of discipline and of order. They were
all so full of life that some were boasting, and they had to be told,
'The spirits of the prophets are subject to the prophets.' You did not
have to plead with them to come to church; you did not have to plead
with them to take part in prayer, or to give an experience or an
exposition, or tell of something that had happened in their experience. No, they all wanted to; they enjoyed it. They wanted to share;
they wanted others to have it. And so the great problem was the
problem of control and of discipline. And yet this is the glory of life

in the Spirit, that you can have liveliness and control at the same time. There is no riot, there is no excess, but there is the divine orderliness — life maintaining itself to the glory of God.

These are the only things that matter. At the beginning they were but a handful of people, as it were. Numbers do not matter finally. What matters is that we correspond to this picture. The early church was but a handful of people; but because of the life that was in it, and the power of the Spirit upon it, it was mighty. It shook the ancient world; it did indeed 'bring down every high thing that was exalting itself against the knowledge of God and the obedience of Christ'.

Well, there are the characteristics of the church. Do we belong to the church? Do we share this life, do we share in this unity?

4.
Sound an alarm

In the address which the Doctor gave at Liverpool in 1968 (see chapter 3) he quoted the text, 'If the trumpet give an uncertain sound, who shall prepare himself to the battle?' On 29 October 1969 he took up that verse of Scripture at the next BEC conference. This was held at Westminster Chapel and once again a very large congregation gathered to hear him speak. He had just recovered from his illness and so this was a particularly emotional occasion, as his reference to himself as 'Paul the aged' indicates.

I regard it as a great honour once more to be asked to speak at the closing rally of the British Evangelical Council. I speak as 'Paul the aged', but I am very glad that the message is still the same. This evening I want to justify the BEC in its stand for certain specific matters. I do this because I find that there is great misunderstanding here and in other countries with regard to it. Indeed, there are those who regard it as an almost criminal institution and feel that some of us are guilty of dividing evangelical people.

I was told by a man in America with whom I preached a few months ago that an evangelist from this country had said to him, with regret, that I was the devil's instrument in Great Britain at the present time because I was dividing evangelical people. That means that there is some misunderstanding somewhere! I am not concerned, of course, about the personal aspect of this charge, but I am a little perplexed about the mentality of an evangelist who charges a man with dividing evangelicals simply because that man appealed for evangelical unity. I stand for evangelical unity — and so does the British Evangelical Council.

You will have noticed that there is a disagreement between evangelicals at the present time. For the purpose of my discussion, I am assuming that all who claim to be evangelical are what they profess to be. However, there are some of us who believe that the World Council of Churches has introduced a new element into the situation which calls for a definite stand on our part. This is where this division comes, and it has been opened up by the World Council of Churches.

But there is something which I want to make plain to you. We honour and respect evangelicals who disagree with us. We do not criticize them as individuals. We do not impute wrong motives to them. We grant that they are as sincere as we are and as honest as we are, and that they believe the gospel as we believe it. What, then, causes the difference? Well, the difference arises at this point. We interpret what they and we are agreed about as indicating that we should take a definite stand against the World Council of Churches and its teaching, and that for the following simple reason: we believe that the World Council and the great world church that it is hoping to form is going to be the greatest hindrance of all to the preaching of this gospel and the salvation of the souls of men and women.

Let us be clear about this. We are concerned about principles, and personalities therefore should not enter in. We, in the British Evangelical Council, hold the view that not only can we do nothing to further the work of the World Council of Churches, but that we are called upon to oppose and resist it with all the might and strength and power that God gives us. This evening, I want to justify that position to you and I am going to do so by means of a well-known statement of the apostle Paul, found in the first epistle to the Corinthians, chapter 14 and verse 8: 'If the trumpet gives an uncertain sound, who shall prepare himself to the battle?'

I am going to expound the position and the attitude of the British Evangelical Council to you in the terms of that statement. Why are we opposed to the ecumenism which is represented by the ecumenical movement? Because we realize that we are in the midst of a very great battle and that the greatest tragedy of the hour is the confusion of the Christian church with regard to it. The condition referred to in the text — 'If the trumpet gives an uncertain sound, who shall prepare himself for the battle?' — is the precise one by which we are confronted. The trumpet is yielding an uncertain sound. I am hoping to show you that we are face to face with one of the greatest battles in the long history of the church, and indeed in the long history of the human race. And I believe that confusion over this is what is paralysing the activities of Christian people at the present time.

Confusion in the church

Now let us look at the two aspects of this matter. Is there anyone in any doubt, I wonder, as to whether confusion exists? Well, nobody should be, because it is being admitted openly. There has been an interesting correspondence recently in *The Times* on this very matter, and if you are not clear about the confusion, then listen to something that was written by the Bishop of Whitby. He says, 'Those of us in responsible positions in the church must feel humbled that it is today in no condition to make any effective stand against the steady erosion of our moral standards.' He admits this with shame and feels that it is largely due first to the preoccupation of the church with her own organization, and secondly, that the clergy, who are largely responsible for the vitality of the church, are confused and shaken by the unceasing attacks on the basic truths of Christian belief. These seem to be cutting the ground from under their feet and so blunting the cutting edge of their message and ministry.

Is the bishop not absolutely right? But, note what he did not say. He did not say that the attack which is undermining the very foundations of the faith of the church is coming from some of the leaders of the church herself! It is not an attack that is only coming from the world; it is an attack from within the church herself and by some of her own leaders. Here is one perfect example of the confusion. What does the bishop propose to do about it? He says, 'The challenge to the church is clear but the time is short, and the call is for immediate action.' But what action? It is: 'We must institute at once, and as top priority at every level, an urgent campaign of church-wide study of the validity and meaning of our faith and of its relevance and application to the present state of society.'

There is an example of the chaos facing us. He says that the church is confused. But what are we to do? We are to set up commissions to study what is the real Christian faith and its validity in the present situation. Have you ever known such bankruptcy? Another writing in the same context agreed that this was a correct diagnosis, and that what the Bishop of Whitby called for was right. That writer went on to say that he was happy to be able to announce that a large and significant conference was already arranged for 1970 to meet in York University to deal with these precise questions — namely as to what the Christian faith is, and what its relevance is to the present issue.

Now there are two prominent spokesmen for the Christian church. What are we to say about this? Well, it is interesting, you notice, that they are beginning to see that their preoccupation with church unity and the ecumenical movement is paralysing their message with regard to the moral state of this country. But are we comforted by this? I am afraid that, for one, I am not. You see, what is being proposed is that you set up a committee to enquire into what is the message of the church. But they had one just before the last world war. They called it 'Towards the conversion of England'.

Commissions are always being set up to discover what the faith is, what our message is, and in the meantime the world goes from bad to worse. My friends, let us be clear about this. A church that has to set up commissions of enquiry to discover what our faith is, is a travesty of the Christian church. As we were told so movingly by Mr Leith Samuel, the truth has been delivered; it is here in front of us. You do not need to set up a commission. The truth is here; it is available. But the tragedy is that the church has become uncertain of her own message.

Well, now, there is one admission of this very confusion, but there are some who go even further than that. I read in a paper, under the heading of 'Wesley's pulpit', the following statement by a preacher. He gave his confession of faith and said, 'I believe in one church, and that church is mankind. Everybody belongs to one church. Mankind is the church.' He then informed his readers that they would not hear biblical or theological language from him and went on to tell them what he was going to say. As far as I am concerned, I still am not clear of what that was. He was quite right in saying that it was neither biblical nor theological, but what it was I am unable to report to you.

Confusion caused by evangelicals

I hope that you see that this is just typical of the present situation. It
is not surprising to us, is it, that non-evangelical people should be in
that condition? It is what we expect from them, holding the position
that they do. That is why evangelicals are evangelical, and for that
very reason there have been evangelicals in the church for centuries.
But what is amazing to us, and what we cannot understand, is how
any evangelicals choose to remain in denominations, churches or
institutions that are in that parlous position, and do not long to come
together with all of us who are agreed upon the faith and to declare
it with a holy boldness. That is the problem. That is where we find
it difficult to understand our brothers. So I must show you some of
the ways in which evangelical people are guilty today of causing this
confusion and are responsible for the trumpet's yielding an uncertain sound.

There are some evangelicals who even glory in this and defend
it. I read an article some time last year, the title of which was 'In
defence of ambiguity'. The author, an evangelical, defended ambiguity and said it was a good thing. What was he talking about?
Well, he was defending certain things which had happened in his
denomination. What were these?

One of them was a new form of communion service which had
been introduced and was known as 'Series 2'. In it was a statement
about what happened to the elements in the communion service. The
evangelicals understood this as meaning that the elements were not
being offered to God. The Anglo-Catholics read it and said it did
mean that. Well, that is the kind of thing this brother was defending
— a formula, a statement which two groups of people can look at,
interpret in diametrically opposite ways and yet claim to be agreed
about. And he was glorying in it!

The same thing is true about a statement in the burial service
which Anglo-Catholics say means praying for the dead. Evangelicals, looking at the same statement, say that it does not. But they
both rejoice in this, that at last they have found a formula that they
can both agree on, though their interpretations are diametrically
opposed. How can they glory in this ambiguity? Why do they do so?
Because it holds the church together. One says it is praying for the
dead; the other says it is not. 'Marvellous,' they say. 'We are both
being kept together and we are saying something.' But what kind of

a sound is being made? 'If the trumpet yield an uncertain sound, who shall prepare himself for the battle?'

Or take this question of the Anglo-Methodist union about which we have been hearing and reading so much. You will remember that it has come to nothing for the time being. Why? The trouble was over the service of reconciliation. What was the matter with that? Well, the problem was that the evangelicals said that this service of reconciliation meant that the Methodist ministers were being reordained, and they objected to that. The Anglo-Catholics also objected to it, but what was the reason for their objection? It was that the statement was not making it sufficiently plain and clear that the Methodist ministers were being reordained. But you see, the authorities who have drawn up the statement, and the leaders of both denominations who tried to put it through, were feeling that they had achieved something extraordinarily wonderful. Why? Well, they had got a formula about which everyone was supposed to agree, but concerning which there were two diametrically opposed interpretations.

They glory in such ambiguity. Some of them put it even like this, that here is a statement which can be followed, but God alone knows what it means. One man can take one view and another can take a diametrically opposed view. My friends, all I am here to assert is this — is it surprising that the people are in a state of confusion? If leaders of the church can foster this kind of uncertainty, what are we to expect from the people as we face this tremendous hour? I can do nothing better at this point than to read to you some words by the Rev. W. A. Harvey, Bishop of Ballarat in Australia. I cannot improve on this. He wrote, 'Most formulas framed as a basis of an act of reunion seem to have only one hope of acceptance by both parties, namely deliberate ambiguity. Each party agreed to the same words but meant something different by it. Where imprecision of meaning is deliberately used so as to cover up real and important differences in order to give an appearance of agreement, one can only call it downright dishonesty.' Is he not right? It is because we say he is right that we belong to the British Evangelical Council. Deliberate ambiguity is in the last analysis nothing but sheer dishonesty.

But there are evangelical brethren with whom we in the BEC are in disagreement who do not glory in this. They regret it, and yet I suggest that they are as guilty of causing this uncertainty, quite as much as the others, though they do it unconsciously. Let me show you some of the ways in which good evangelical brethren are increasing this uncertainty at the present time.

Some of them do it, you know, by adopting an attitude of neutrality to the World Council of Churches. They say, 'We are not for and we are not against.' They are neutral. This appears to be a very Christian, charitable attitude until you begin to examine it. We must bear in mind that the World Council of Churches is deliberately based on doctrinal indifferentism. Their formulæ have to be sufficiently vague to include the Eastern Orthodox Church on the one hand and evangelicals on the other. Now surely to be neutral to such a process, which is framed to produce one great world church, including the Roman Catholic Church, is indeed ultimately to condone it. There is no neutrality possible in the light of the New Testament on such a matter. Did you notice in the Scripture that our Lord says that the tree is either good or bad; it is never half and half? The prophet is either a true prophet, or else he is a false prophet. The fruit is either good, or else it is bad. Neutrality is never commended in the New Testament.

The people noticed this in our Lord's preaching, and they said, 'This man speaketh with authority and not as the scribes.' What was the teaching of the scribes like? Oh, they were the men who would argue about minutiæ. They could explain almost everything and they had their modifications and qualifications. Nobody could understand them and people just had to follow them blindly. Our Lord was clear. He was plain. He spoke with authority. A thing is either good or bad. You cannot be neutral; it is impossible.

There are other evangelicals who become involved in this uncertainty in a rather different way, but one which is quite common at the present time. These say that their confessional statements and basis of faith are right, and as long as they remain, that seems in their opinion to cover everything. But here, I think, there is very real confusion. What the Christian church is teaching at any given time is what is being proclaimed from its pulpits and not what is handed down on paper. I told you this in another connection at Liverpool last year and I have to come back to it again.

The idea seems to be that as long as the confession of faith is correct then it does not matter very much what is being currently said. But surely the teaching of the church is what is being preached. That is what the people are hearing. Here are the people waiting for the sound of the trumpet. Are they being called to battle or not? Well now, it is no use saying to them that there is something written in a book somewhere. They do not read books, but they come and listen to the preaching and the statement of the ministers — and they take that to be the teaching of the church.

I wonder what we would say when we go to a symphony concert, expecting to hear something enjoyable and pleasurable, but what we actually hear from the orchestra is some terrible cacophony of clashes and discords — noise and clatter and bang. I wonder what we would say if, when we had made our protest, the conductor stood before us at the end and said, 'All the players have got the right score in front of them.' That does not help us, does it? We are not interested in the correctness of the score. We go there to enjoy the music. It is no argument, therefore, to say that as long as your formula is correct then all is well. It is what is being said that is important. This distinction between paper statements and what is literally preached and taught is one of the most specious and dangerous arguments which is being used at this present time.

Another way in which our brethren are causing confusion is as follows. Though they themselves believe and say the right things — and there is no question about this at all — they belong to denominations which as a whole deny the very things that they are teaching. Now the people see that. And what do they make of it? Well, they hear a man standing for the evangelical faith, but then they find that he belongs to a church in which some of the leaders are almost denying the faith and denouncing it and ridiculing it. What are the people to say? What can they make of it? What is the sound that is coming to them from such a trumpet? There are many who are doing this.

I met a man again this last summer, a Presbyterian minister in the United States. He was a good evangelical man, and I said to him, 'How do you justify remaining in your denomination after the 1967 confession has been approved?' 'Ah', he said, 'we do not believe that.' 'My dear friend,' I replied, 'you are a Presbyterian and your church has accepted this officially. You cannot be a Presbyterian when it suits you and then an independent when it suits you. You are either a Presbyterian or you are not.' You see, he was justifying his position in terms of independency while he was a Presbyterian.

That is the kind of confusion in the minds of the ministers, and it leads to confusion in the minds of the people. Another way in which people do this quite innocently is simply by marching with

people who do not agree with our evangelical doctrine. These joint
marches on Good Friday and other days are a new feature in our
church, are they not? All march together from Trafalgar Square to
the Roman Catholic Cathedral. What is the man in the street, who
sees this great procession of all the religious denominations, the
Roman Catholics included, and led by the Salvation Army band, to
make of this? Can he be in anything but a state of confusion?

I was so disturbed about this a year or two back when it happened
here in Westminster, that I wrote to the then General of the Salvation
Army and protested. The reply I got from him was that they took part
in order to bear their witness. He used this argument. He said, 'What
we do when we march in such a procession with our band is exactly
the same thing as we do when we go and sell copies of the *War Cry*
in public houses.' Now do you see the fallacy of that argument? I had
to point out to him that when they go to a public house they are
dealing with unbelievers, but when they march in that procession
they are marching with liberals, modernists, Roman Catholics,
Anglo-Catholics — men who deny the gospel by their teaching. It
was a church procession, whereas the other was a form of evangelism to unbelievers. The public house is not a church, but when
you march with these others it is the church that is giving a public
demonstration.

What is someone to say as he looks at all this? Does not the
question, 'What does the church stand for?' inevitably arise? Is it the
Salvation Army teaching, or is it the Roman Catholic teaching?
Thus men who want this church union are causing confusion. I can
understand everybody else wanting this kind of union, but what I
cannot understand is that evangelical men should say that they long
to be united with these liberal bodies who deny the very essence of
the faith.

There is another way in which confusion is being promoted, and
I am coming to the end of this rather sorry list. There are those who
are just saying nothing. These are the people who claim to be ultra-
spiritual. Their claim is that they are always positive. They never
denounce anything. They are much too nice for that; they are much
too loving. They are always preaching a positive gospel. They never
criticize wrong teaching; they never say that they are against
anything at all. They are just doing their own work and preaching a
positive gospel. What is the answer to them?

Well, this is how Luther answered them: 'He therefore is a faithful shepherd who not only feeds but also guards the sheep. This is done when he finds out heresies and errors.' There are grievous wolves and darkness. Listen to the apostle Paul, warning the church at Ephesus when he gave that word of farewell to the elders at the seashore. He knew that wolves were going to come in, these false teachers, and he warned them and he taught them. A shepherd who does not guard and protect his sheep is in the last analysis a hireling. Shepherds not only feed, but guard and protect the flock. Never was there a greater need of such a ministry than at this present time.

The battle

Very well, my friends, there are some of the ways in which I believe many good men today are quite unconsciously augmenting the uncertain note and sound that is given by the trumpet. What, of course, makes this so tragic and serious is the battle in which we are engaged. 'If the trumpet gives an uncertain sound, who shall prepare him for the battle?'

And the battle is hot and strong. Do we not realize this? What is being fought over? Well, the great battle today is for the whole of the Christian faith. It is being queried, denied and ridiculed almost as never before. Is this a time for neutrality? Is this a time for uncertainty? Is this a time for compromise? The Christian faith is what is at stake! But the man in the street does not know this. I have often said, and I will say it again, that I am not surprised that the masses of the people are outside the Christian church at this present time. How can they know what Christianity is if they get their impressions of it only from the television, the radio and from their newspapers? And then what a contradiction exists between the Christian church and Christianity itself! That is the very essence of this whole trouble.

Consider also the great battle for the church. What is the Christian church? Indeed, is there any need for a church? There are many today who will say we do not need the Christian church as an institution any longer. There are others who are advocating a churchless Christianity. There are those who are telling us to do almost anything except come to church. We are to bear our witness in the world, we are to show love, we are to go into politics, and so on and so forth. The whole existence of the church is being questioned at this present time. Then does doctrine count? Does it matter what you believe? Does it matter what the church believes? These questions have got to be asked today. The man in the street is asking them. The ordinary member of the church is asking them. Is Rome right after all? You see, if you march with them you are more or less saying that it is, are you not?

And that raises another question. Was the Protestant Reformation a mistake? Should not everybody have stayed in and tried to reform the church? Was Luther wrong? Ah, but, you say, he was thrown out. Yes, but if you do things that make it certain that you will be thrown out, you are really going out. And John Calvin was not thrown out, he went out — and so have great leaders throughout the centuries. These are the questions which we have to ask. Can two walk together except they be agreed? No! Let me read you a statement by a prominent Roman Catholic in Northern Ireland. He seems to me to have put this very plainly and very clearly, as reported in a paper in this country on 29th August. Cardinal William Plumley, after speaking to Mr Callaghan when he visited Northern Ireland, put it like this, and surely we can totally agree with him. 'Bible Protestants' he said, 'have no common meeting place with the Catholic Church and never will have.' Well then, I ask each soul, how can you march with them, and how can you have a joint service with them? How can you go to their places and invite them into your pulpits? Here is a Roman Catholic stating the matter quite plainly. Cardinal Heenan has done so as well.

There has been no doctrinal change in Rome towards an evangelical Protestant position — none whatever. But people do not seem to be aware of this at the present time. It is all because, of course, the official spokesmen of the Roman church have changed their tactics. They are more friendly. They do not denounce us any more. They call us separated brethren. But remember that our Lord dealt with that kind of situation. He said, 'They come to you in sheep's clothing but inwardly they are ravening wolves.' I preferred them when they came undisguised, but now they are coming in sheep's clothing, and unwary, untaught, evangelical people are saying there is a great change in Rome. One of the greatest authorities of the ecumenical movement, Bishop Stephen Neill, has said that in one respect, a social one, Rome is nearer to us than she has been — that is to say, in her friendliness of approach and so on. But he added, and again quite truly, that doctrinally she is actually further away from us now than she was before the Protestant Reformation.

Now there is a man who, though he believes in the ecumenical movement and the World Council, honestly acknowledges the facts of the situation. So, you see, we are engaged in this great battle, and you have got to face this, my friends. Can you be neutral about this? Are you neutral on this question of Rome and the worship of Mary? The pope has asked people during the month of October to pray to Mary in particular. Is that all right? Is it unimportant?

This is the battle in which we are engaged. We do not want to be fighting; we would much prefer to go on with our work. But while these changes are occurring and people are drifting, it surely behoves us to stand and speak and to let people know something of what is really taking place. So we are in a great battle for the whole future of the Christian church.

But there is also this tremendous battle for the souls of men. Never was there such a fight. There is a great need for evangelism, for bringing people to conversion. But how can this be done? If the trumpet gives an uncertain sound, can anyone be converted? But the sound is uncertain. It is no use evangelicals in the denominations which belong to the World Council of Churches saying, 'But I preach the true gospel.' 'Yes,' says the man who is listening, 'I know what you say, but I notice you belong to the same church as a man who says the exact opposite. Who am I to believe? Am I to believe you, my local minister, or am I to believe the great leaders of your denomination?'

Questions that we must ask

There are questions that have got to be answered before you can engage in true evangelism. What are these? 'What is the truth about the natural man? Has he fallen or is he rising? Is he just a reasoning animal, or was he originally made in the image and likeness of God? What is man?' Alas, there is an awful uncertainty and lack of clarity today with regard to this very question. And, as I have shown you, it is not enough that you should say the right thing if you belong to the same church as a man who says the exact opposite. The man in the pew is hearing an uncertain note on the trumpet.

And then you have to ask another question. Is there such a thing as the wrath of God against all ungodliness and self-righteousness of men, or is Paul's teaching on that just Jewish, rabbinic? Then you have to ask the question, is there such a place as hell? Ah, but I must be careful. I notice that the Lord Chancellor said, 'Women are to be warned to contact their doctor immediately if their husbands become suddenly depressed, and especially if they suddenly start talking about God and about hell.' The Lord Chancellor of England! 'The moment you find your husband talking about God and hell, send for the doctor'! There are doctors and doctors!

But these are the questions, my friends. And who is Christ? Is he just a man? That is what many would say, even the majority. Just a man — Jesus. That is what they always call him. They do not refer to him as the Lord Jesus Christ. But is he only a man? And what has he done? What is the meaning of that death of his on the cross? Is he just a supreme pacifist, or was he giving his life a ransom for many? Is there certainty about this? Is the trumpet giving a certain sound? Can anyone be converted in the midst of all this confusion? Is regeneration a fact, or is it some psychological, pathological condition? Is there to be a second coming of the Lord of glory?

Moral decline

But lest somebody might think that I belong to a particular political party, let me remind you that we are living in a country in which the Deputy Leader of the Opposition and his wife state publicly that they are proud of their daughter when she gives birth to an illegitimate child. *Proud* of her! Thank God, I say, that they did not turn her out! We would all applaud them if they showed love to her, but we have reached the stage when men and women seem to be saying, 'Evil, be thou my good.' *Proud* of her! We are faced with one of the most terrible moral collapses that this country of ours has ever known. That battle is raging all around us.

And you know, my friends, that it is the Christian church, and only the church, that has always dealt with such decline. I can prove this to you quite clearly from history. The best and the most moral

periods in the history of this country have always been those that
have followed reformations and revival. Think of the Elizabethan
era, the Puritan era, and the era that followed the Evangelical
Awakening. This has been invariable, and it has happened in other
countries too. So, as it were, the world outside can only look to the
church, waiting for a certain note, waiting for authority. And to me
it is more than deplorable that the head of the legal system in this
country should speak in the way that he did.

We are confronted by lawlessness. We are confronted by these
unofficial strikes by unions, students and children which may
threaten the whole life and livelihood of this country. It is sheer
lawlessness. In every realm and department of life men are breaking
the rules and justifying themselves. Why is all this taking place? The
only answer is that men and women no longer believe in God.
Whenever you cease to believe in God, you always get lawlessness.
There will never be a return to a belief in law, even as a general
concept, until men and women return to the Supreme Lawgiver.
Surely every lawyer would start by saying that you must have
authority. Everyone must not be left to do what he or she wishes and
chooses. Authority is necessary for life and the ultimate authority is
God. Yet, the Lord Chancellor tells people to be a bit alarmed about
the mental stability of people when they talk about God. He
condemns and indeed he ridicules and rejects the only hope of
producing law and order and decent living in this country. That is the
battle in which we are engaged.

But the supreme tragedy of all is this, that at a time when
everything else is failing, and men and women perhaps are beginning to look wistfully in the direction of the Christian church when
faced with this moral chaos, what do they find? Well, they find
leaders in the Christian church supporting the change in the law with
regard to homosexuality and divorce and abortion. They find a
leader in one section of the Christian church saying that all this is a
sign of adolescence, that we are no longer babes. We have left
behind the relics of Puritanism. I do not know whether you have
realized that what we are passing through is only adolescence! That
must mean that we have not yet reached maturity! What that is going
to be like I cannot imagine. But this is adolescence and we are
advancing! And the same speaker entered a witness box and gave
evidence in favour of the publishers of *Lady Chatterley's Lover*. A
leader of the church! Is it surprising that the people say, 'What does

80   *Unity in truth*

law and morality matter? I can do what I like, what I want to do.'
When you get leaders speaking like this, what do you expect from
the people?

What is the church doing?

Or let me show you another aspect of this whole condition, to which
our evangelical brethren who do not belong to this council are
contributing. At a time like this, with this terrible battle that is going
on round about us, what is the Christian church doing? She is
preoccupied with trivialities. What has she been arguing about
during the last two years? The validity of holy orders, and minute
changes in ritual and ceremonial. What is the church arguing about?
Oh, the strict inviolability of episcopacy. There has been a great
conference in Rome recently with the world on fire and going to hell,
and what have they been arguing about? The precise power of the
pope. My dear friends, you have heard about Nero fiddling while
Rome was burning, have you not? The Christian church is doing
something still more tragic at the present time. Episcopal hands are
regarded as essential to the church. The strict inviolability of
episcopacy; the power of the pope, and all these utter trivialities —
while the world is in agony and men and women are dying around
us, without a hope to cheer the tomb.

   And I regret to have to go on to this last point, but it is true. The
apparent moral duplicity of these ministers of the Christian church
is increasing the confusion. What is needed in this country, and most
countries, at the present time is a return to honesty, to integrity, to
truth, to your word meaning what it says without any ambiguity.
And what is the church revealing? An appearance of a unity which
does not exist in fact.

   The denominations today are not united, any one of them. They
have all got their sects and sections. They hold together simply to
keep the body together. It is a fraud, it is a sham, it is not true — and
the man outside knows this. They recognize on paper the ancient
creeds, but they are honest enough to tell us sometimes that they do
not believe them. Well, how can you recognize them and at the same
time deny their teaching? The people are looking on and they see
men taking solemn vows, but at the same time having mental
reservations. Some of them even say openly in their ordination

sermons that they do not believe the things which they have just vowed to teach and support. This moral duplicity is not only confusing the people. It is doing something worse. It is increasing this lawlessness that is spreading in such a terrible manner. It is no use our saying that unity is the essential thing, and that without it we are lost, and then to turn it down because of some triviality such as episcopacy and episcopal ordination.

The world can see through us and see that we recognize no fixed, clear authority. How can a church that is guilty of ambiguity give a certain call to honesty, to stability, to truth, to righteousness, to a submission to law and to standards? How can she do it when she herself is in her life a denial of her own message? How do you expect the world to listen if the church at one and the same time is saying 'yes' and 'no' about the same thing?

Why do I belong to the British Evangelical Council? Why do my brethren? It is because I cannot say 'yes' and 'no' at the same time. And why not? Well, because I take my stand with the apostle Paul when he puts it like this: 'For the Son of God, Jesus Christ who was preached among you by us, by me and Silvanus and Timotheus, was not yea and nay, but in him was yea. For all the promises of God in him are yea, and in him Amen, unto the glory of God by us.' There is no ambiguity, no uncertainty in the united apostolic proclamation — one faith delivered once and for ever to the saints.

Sound an alarm

What, then, is the need at a time like this? What is the church, what is the world waiting for? As I see it, it is the command that I find coming to me out of this book as I read it day by day, month by month and year by year. Sound an alarm! Sound an alarm — ere it be too late! Not compromises, ambiguity, equivocation! Not modifications or qualifications, nor anything just to preserve an institution! No, no! Look at the people, have a heart of compassion, see where they are going. Sound an alarm. 'Lift up thy voice with strength. Be not afraid, say unto the cities of Judah, Behold your God.'

And what is the call? 'Cry aloud, cry aloud' — with no uncertainty. 'Spare not, lift up thy voice like a trumpet and show the people their transgressions and the house of Jacob their sin.' If ever there was a need for that, it is now. And it is no use your saying, 'I am an evangelical, I am doing this,' if you belong to a church that is denying it. The trumpet is yielding an uncertain sound, and nobody is preparing himself for any sort of battle.

We must say this together, and we need a voice that will wake the very dead. We need to cry aloud and to sound this alarm. This was the glory of the apostles, was it not? We read that Peter stood up on the Day of Pentecost with the eleven and he lifted up his voice. He denounced them, and then preached the glorious gospel to them. The apostle Paul did the same in Athens. This country is so similar at the present time to that city. He went before them and he said, 'Whom ye ignorantly worship, him declare I unto you.' We must declare the whole counsel of God without fear or favour, without equivocation and without uncertainty.

I belong to the British Evangelical Council because it stands for and is trying to do this. But if you would like to know my final reason for belonging to it, it is this: I know that a day is coming in my history (some of you wondered whether it had come eighteen months ago), but a day is coming in my history and in yours when the trumpet shall sound and the dead shall rise, and you and I will be amongst them. That will not be an uncertain sound! That will be the blast from God, from the holy angels. They will take the trumpet and it will sound. The dead will arise, and you and I will be amongst them. We must all appear before the judgement throne of Christ and give an account of the deeds done in the body, whether good or bad.

Therefore, knowing the terror of the Lord, am I to mute the sound of this trumpet so that I can join with others on exactly the opposite basis for the sake of a little peace and popularity? No, no! I shall have to appear before him and give an account of the deeds done in the body, whether good or bad. Therefore, knowing the terror of the Lord, we persuade men, not modifying the truth or joining with its foes, for my dear friends, if ever there was a need for a clear trumpet blast, it is now. Let us join together, let us dedicate ourselves together, to see that the trumpet gives a certain sound — a clarion call to repentance and faith in the Lord Jesus Christ, and to the establishment of New Testament churches, plain and clear and obvious to all men. Let us stand for the truths of God in the midst of this wicked and perverse generation.

So 'Who is on the Lord's side?' Let him declare it; let him be ready to suffer for it. Who is on the Lord's side? Let it be seen where you are. 'If the Lord be God, follow him: but if Baal, then follow him.' If you believe that the church of the New Testament is an evangelical church, stand with it plainly and clearly. But if you want just a territorial church that includes everybody, a church that is the whole of mankind, well I say, go to it. But let it be clear where you stand.

Be a man! Acquit yourselves as men! Be strong! Stand fast in the faith! 'If the trumpet yields an uncertain sound, who shall prepare him for the battle?' But if we declare the Son of God, who is not yea and nay, but the everlasting yea of God to all the needs of the individual soul and the needs of the whole world — well, then men and women can be expected to turn to him and to fall down at his feet, and eventually in glory to cast their crowns before him, lost in wonder, love and praise.

5.
The Mayflower Pilgrims

In 1970, the Doctor spoke twice under the auspices of the BEC. In addition to the annual conference (see next address) a special public rally was held on 1 October in Westminster Chapel. Its purpose was to commemorate the 450th anniversary of the sailing of the Pilgrim Fathers to the New World. The Doctor had referred to these men when speaking on Luther.

It was the Doctor himself who provided the stimulus for the meeting. He had learned that Dr Charles Woodbridge was to be in Europe at that time and it was resolved that he should be invited to speak. Dr Woodbridge had successfully completed a doctoral thesis at Princeton and held the chair in Church History at Fuller Seminary. He had been a staunch colleague of Rev. Gresham Machen.

I must take just a moment in which to express my great sense of privilege at being present here this evening in this great gathering. It is an encouraging sight to see so many people who realize that the great event which we are remembering together is something that should be commemorated.

It is also a particular pleasure for me to be sharing this meeting and speaking with Dr Charles Woodbridge. I have known of him for a number of years. Mr Caiger told you just a little about him and his distinguished career as a Professor of Church History. However, he did not tell you that, unlike many professors of church history, our distinguished guest is not merely one of those theoretical, academic historians who can write and speak learnedly about the glories of the past. He is also a man who has in his own life put into practice what he teaches and preaches. In the early thirties of this century, he stood with the great Dr Gresham Machen in that epic and notable fight in the Presbyterian Church in the north of the United States and was excommunicated with Dr Machen and others. If ever a man, therefore, had a right to speak on the Pilgrim Fathers that man is Dr Woodbridge, and that is even more important than the fact that his forebears landed in the United States in 1634. He is a pilgrim himself by conviction and has proved this by his action. We, therefore, honour him as a visitor to our country and thank God that he was able to come and to join us in this celebration service.

Now, why did a number of us feel that this notable event in the history of the human race and of the church should be commemorated? If we had no other reason for doing so, it is because it is one of the great epic stories of all history and it is good to be reminded in these flabby, easy-going days of men of character and strength, conviction and stature. One of the American poets has put this strikingly in very well-known words:

> Lives of great men all remind us
> We can make our lives sublime
> And departing leave behind us
> Footprints on the sands of time.
> Footprints that perhaps another
> Sailing o'er life's solemn main,
> A forlorn and shipwrecked brother,
> Seeing may take heart again.

So I believe that as we continue to look together at the footprints of these Pilgrim Fathers and their sons in New England, we shall, under the blessing of Almighty God, take heart again and resolve to go forward in the fight.

Why we should study church history

I am particularly interested in this commemoration because, in a most extraordinary manner, there is a very close parallel between what happened in those early days of the seventeenth century and what is happening today. This is why it seems to me that one of the most important things for all Christians to do at the present time is to study church history, and particularly this period. Why? Well because it was an age of transition and ours is as well. Everybody is agreed about this. The period of the Renaissance, the Reformation and a century or so afterwards was one of those great climactic points in the history of the whole human race.

You and I are in a similar situation and notwithstanding all its problems and difficulties, it is a privilege to be alive at this time. We are involved in one of those great turning-points of history and, as I see it, it is a most astonishing and remarkable thing that, as members of the Christian church, we are confronted by precisely the same question as confronted those men 350 years ago and more. Now, what is that? Well, the great question confronting them and us is the nature of the Christian church and the character of Christian worship. That is what the crisis then was all about and that, as we have been reminded, is the great question which faces us today.

The great value of church history is that it not only presents us with doctrine — and that is all-important and primary — but it also concentrates on its practical application. Many people fail at this point. They may be correct in their doctrines, but they never apply them. They are theorists. Their attitude is entirely objective. It seems to me, however, that the moment you read history and are confronted with what people actually did, you are compelled to ask yourself the question: 'What am I doing about what I believe?'

Another particular gain from church history, as I see it, and of this history about which we are concerned tonight, is that we are called upon to think. May I interject here that I am one of those who does not fear to say that in some respects I am grateful for the ecumenical movement. Let me explain what I mean by that lest I be excommunicated immediately. What I mean is that this movement has thrown all the major denominations into a melting-pot situation. They say so themselves. Very well, I think that is a good thing because it should compel all Christians to think these things through once more. Of course, we should think in a different way from the ecumenical people and arrive at a different conclusion. But I am grateful in days like these for anything that even helps us to think because the main trouble is that people will not do so. They are content to rest with what they were brought up in, and in their indolence and laziness they will not face the issues. In this age of transition, everything is undergoing reconsideration and we are therefore being required to face challenging questions.

A further benefit of studying history is that we can look at how issues were faced in the past and become aware, not only of some of the dangers godly men have faced, but also of some of the errors into which even they have fallen. This is what we are going to do with the Pilgrim Fathers and we will find that even they were not perfect.

Who were the Pilgrim Fathers?

It seems important to me that we spend at least a moment in an exact definition concerning these Pilgrim Fathers. People are no longer aware of church history and they do not understand these things. Dr Woodbridge has painted in the essentials for us. In the sixteenth century a reformation of the church took place in this country but immediately there were some who were not satisfied with it. In effect they said, 'We have reformed the doctrine but we have not carried the reformation right through in our church practice and government.' And they began to agitate about this. These were the people who were called Puritans. They felt that the reformation was incomplete and that in this country it had not been carried through with the same thoroughness as it had in most of the European countries and nations.

But unfortunately a division developed even amongst these Puritans — not immediately, but from about 1562 to the end of the century. Three main groups emerged. There were those who believed in staying in the Church of England with the aim of bringing pressure to bear, trusting that things would gradually be improved and they would obtain a complete reformation. But then others soon appeared who were not content with this. They said that a different form of church government must be immediately introduced. For instance, there was a man like Thomas Cartwright, who was in many ways the first Presbyterian. He was ejected from his post as Professor of Divinity in the University of Cambridge in 1570 because he was teaching Presbyterian rather than Episcopalian principles. Well, there was that group. They did not believe in separating from the state, nor did they believe in separating from the church. But they wanted to turn the Church of England from an Episcopalian church into a Presbyterian church on the lines Calvin laid down for the church in Geneva. Another group arose. These were men who said, 'We must leave the church immediately and not wait. This is all wrong.' They were led by a man called Robert Browne and were known as the Brownists. In many ways, he was the originator of Congregationalism and Independency. Yet another group began to appear. These agreed substantially with Browne but thought that it was not necessary to leave the Church of England because Congregational churches could be formed within it.

It is indeed important that we should know something about this history. All the Puritans were agreed with what John Foxe, the great martyrologist, stated. He said that there were still remnants of popery left in the Church of England which he wished God would remove, for God knew that they were the cause of much blindness and strife. Foxe pleaded for more conformity to the law of Christ and to primitive Christianity. All to whom I have referred agreed about this but they differed about how further reformation should be pursued.

Their view of the church

Why have I said all this? Because we are confronted by exactly the same situation at the present time. There are people who are equally evangelical who disagree on this point in much the same way as in the sixteenth century. But the great and the basic question of this debate can, in the last analysis, it seems to me, be put like this: are all in every parish who are baptized automatically Christians and members of the Christian church? Was Richard Hooker, whose work on ecclesiastical polity has been the main governing book of the outlook of the Church of England, right when he said that the English state and the Church of England were coextensive? This meant that every baptized person — and by law all were to be baptized — was thereby a Christian. Now is that the right view of the church? Or is the church a body that consists only of gathered saints — not of those who have been baptized, but of those who can be regarded as saints because of the evidence which they give of that fact?

Now, that is still the great issue before us and there are still these two basic views of a Christian church. Are all baptized people Christians and members of the church, or is it only those who can testify to their belief and who give evidence of their regeneration? This was the basic issue then and it is still the great and the basic issue today.

It was, of course, in the light of this that the church was formed in Gainsborough and in Scrooby which spread out to Leyden and further. I am therefore glad that Dr Woodbridge emphasized the fact that these Pilgrim Fathers who left Holland for the reasons he put before us were not revolutionaries. There are people who are interested in the Pilgrim Fathers purely in a political sense, regarding them as politicians, as rebels, as revolutionaries. They were nothing of the sort. They were anxious to go out to form this new land in America which would be a colony of England and they were very anxious to swear their allegiance to James I. There is no question whatsoever but that their main motive in crossing the Atlantic was a religious one and that was furthered and accentuated by the other reasons which have been given to us. The great Dr John Owen, the Puritan, put it perfectly, I think, in these words: 'Multitudes of pious, peaceable Protestants were driven, by the severities of church and state, to leave their native country and seek a refuge for their lives and liberty with freedom for the worship of God in a wilderness in the ends of the earth.' That, undoubtedly, is the reason why they went.

Now what did they establish there? It is important, I think, that we should know that they established Congregational churches. They neither established new branches of the Church of England nor Presbyterian churches. Their beliefs, as we have been reminded, were the beliefs of all Puritans at that time. These men were all Calvinists. Perhaps you did not know that John Robinson, the pastor of these people in Leyden, was a great protagonist of the truth of the Canons of Dort and was greatly respected and admired by the Dutch theologians. He was put up to defend those canons and did so in a very masterly manner. He was a very able and erudite man. His books prove that quite clearly. They all held what we would call the Reformed faith, and that is the truth about every single one of them. I know that there was a mixed multitude on board the *Mayflower*, but I am talking about the people who formed the core of the Pilgrim Fathers.

As a consequence, they had certain rules for the formation of their churches and they were very punctilious about these. You could not just join the church at will. You had to be examined. All members had to make a confession of their faith and to make it clear that they believed the great cardinal articles of this Reformed faith as it had been taught by Luther and Calvin and so on. But in addition to that, they had to subscribe to a particular covenant in order to belong to an individual church because, to them, a church was a gathering of people who, holding certain views, covenanted together to live together, to worship God together so as to make the gospel known. So they covenanted together to do this and no one would be received as a member of the church unless that person signed the covenant.

Another thing for us to note about them is that they had no bishops. They had ministers, elders and deacons, and what is really important is that each church chose and ordained its own minister and admitted and expelled members of the church. No outside body decreed this. You see, it was a real departure from Anglicanism, from Episcopacy, and indeed also from Presbyterianism. It was a Congregational church and the other churches were influenced by them. Now as you read the story of the various emigrations that went out during the following years you will find that many of them went with different and varying ideas, but what has been outlined became the common principle and practice. The New England churches, speaking generally, were Congregational churches.

At this point I would venture on a few criticisms. The Pilgrim Fathers, as I have said just now, were not perfect. They were men of their age and of their own generation, as we are, and this is where we can learn from them. We should note that they attempted to form a theocracy. There is no question about this. Only church members were allowed to vote, for instance, in appointing the officers of the state. There is no question but that they still carried with them certain tyrannical ideas and were not clear upon the relationship between the church and state at that point. It took a number of years for these settlers in America to get clear on this issue in all the various denominations and there is no connection between church and state in America at this present time.

It seems to me that they were also guilty of imagining that the conditions of church membership and church government could be so laid down that the church could continue like that in perpetuity. This, of course, is always the danger that confronts reformers, men who have to start afresh. They have left a particular body because they feel that they have clearly seen its errors. Their danger is to think that they can make it impossible for the church ever to go astray again. They recall that the church which went wrong was right at the beginning, and so a new church has to be safeguarded by definitions to prevent the same thing happening again. They believe they can do that. History, however, has proved that it cannot be done.

I have a particular reason for pointing this out. There are people in this country today who are disturbed about the general situation and about their own denomination. What many of these friends tell me is holding them in their denomination is that they have no guarantee, if they were to leave, that what they form or join will be all right in a hundred years' time. So they stay where they are. Well, both those attitudes are wrong. It is true that we cannot legislate for prosperity, as the Pilgrim Fathers thought. But we must also realize, as they did, that we are responsible to God for our own day and generation. Let us learn both those lessons from the Pilgrim Fathers.

There is a very wonderful statement by John Robinson himself about this, and I want to read it to you. It not only establishes the point which I have just made, but it helps me to deal with an error with regard to him. There is a statement of his which is most frequently quoted by theological liberals and which leads them to think that he is on their side. He made it at the end of his last sermon to the Pilgrim Fathers before they sailed from Holland. Incidentally, he preached on Ezra 8. That was an excellent choice of text for that event, and so let those of us who are preachers learn from it the lesson of preaching suitably to an occasion.

This is how he ended: 'Brethren, we are now quickly to part from one another; and whether I may ever live to see your faces on earth any more, the God of heaven only knows. But whether the Lord have appointed that or no, I charge you before God and before his blessed angels that you follow me no further than you have seen me follow the Lord Jesus Christ. If God reveal anything to you by any other instrument of his, be as ready to receive it as ever you were to receive any truth by my ministry.'

Then he said what is the material phrase: 'For I am verily persuaded, I am very confident *the Lord hath more truth yet to break forth out of his Holy Word.*'

Now it is crucial that we do not stop there for an understanding of his meaning. He continued: 'For my part, I cannot sufficiently bewail the condition of the reformed churches who are come to a period in religion; and will go at present no further than the instruments of their first reformation. The Lutherans cannot be drawn to go beyond what Luther saw: whatever part of his will our good God has imparted and revealed unto Calvin, they will rather die than embrace it. And the Calvinists, you see, stick first where they were left by that great man of God who yet saw not all things.'

What a balanced and sane man this great pastor of the Pilgrim Fathers was! He went on to say, 'This is a misery much to be lamented, for they were "burning and shining lights" in their times, yet they penetrated not into the "whole counsel of God" but were they now living, they would be as willing to embrace further light as that which they first received. I beseech you to remember it — it is an article of your church covenant, "That you will be ready to receive whatever truth shall be made known unto you from the written Word of God". Remember that and every other article of your most sacred covenant. But I must herewithall exhort you to heed what you receive as truth, examine it, consider it, compare it with the other Scriptures of truth, before you do receive it. For it is not possible the Christian world should come so lately out of such thick anti-Christian darkness and that perfection of knowledge should break forth at once.'

What a great and glorious statement! We all need to pay heed to it.

The phrase that is so frequently quoted by liberals is, 'I am verily persuaded, I am very confident the Lord hath more truth yet to break forth out of his Holy Word.' This has become their great keyword. They interpret that statement to mean that it is very wrong of us, as Christians, still to adhere to the Thirty-Nine Articles, or the Westminster Confession of Faith, or the teaching of the Protestant fathers. They claim that because science has developed the whole situation today is different. What those men of the seventeenth century believed was only for their own age. We have more light. That is the kind of thinking which governs their own theological understanding.

It is abundantly clear from the context that John Robinson at this point was talking about one thing only, and that was church government. He was an honest man, you see. There was a time when he had adopted and espoused the teachings of Robert Browne, but having been persuaded by a Congregationalist called Henry Jacob that he was wrong, he modified his opinion. Great men are ready to change their opinions if they can be convinced that they have been wrong! These men were not rigid bigots. They were godly men and they were ready to consider points of view and to evaluate them carefully in the light of the teaching of the Scripture. They were open to conviction and, as John Robinson in effect says so clearly and so excellently, 'Don't imagine that Luther or Calvin in a few years could put everything right. They dealt with these great central fundamental truths of the faith but they had not got the time, apart from anything else, to work out all these other matters.' It is here that he suggests that further light may yet break out from the Scriptures. So if ever you hear anybody again justifying his heterodoxy or liberalism in theology in terms of the statement of John Robinson give him the lie direct and put him right on his facts. [1]

What explains the Pilgrim Fathers?

What, then, is it that explains these Pilgrim Fathers? What is it that led to this epic story? There is no doubt about this answer. It was *their knowledge of God.* Above everything else, they were godly men, sober men. Nobody would ever mistake any one of these men for a film star. They were men who lived under the eye of God and they walked in the fear of the Lord. I told you about their theological views, but these were not held in a merely intellectual manner. They penetrated the very fibre of their being. Their lives were entirely submitted and subordinated to this. They believed also very deeply in God's guidance and in his providential care, even down to the minutest details of their lives. And that, of course, led to their very characteristic view of life. Life to these men was a pilgrimage. This, of course, was the great note of that century. John Bunyan, we know, wrote his *Pilgrim's Progress,* but there were many other men before Bunyan who had written along these same lines. The great secret of these men was that to them the whole of life in this world was nothing but a pilgrimage. They were journeymen in this world.

William Haller, who has written a most excellent book on the *Origins of Puritanism,* uses a very pregnant statement when he says, 'Heaven was theirs already, and if presently they demanded possession of the earth as well, that was no more than human.' That is a profoundly acute and true remark. The men who were mainly concerned about heaven and were assured that they were going there have incidentally been the men who have done the greatest things in this world and have been the pioneers in so many respects. These men, before ever they decided to go to America, were pilgrims towards eternity. They had already been pilgrims on earth for eleven years in Holland before they set sail for America, which was but a further step. If you decide to leave England and to go to Holland because of your principles, well, it is only a little bit further to cross the Atlantic and to go to America. It all depends upon your point of view, and the governing thought of these men was what we find so much emphasized in the epistle to the Hebrews: 'Here have we no continuing city, but we seek one to come.'

They were not interested in affluent societies. They did not talk about settling down in this world and having a good time. No, no! They were strangers and pilgrims; they were travellers and journey-men. They said with Paul, 'Our citizenship is in heaven.' That was their whole view of life. Or as the author of the epistle to the Hebrews puts it, 'These men were looking for a city which had foundations, whose builder and maker is God.' They knew that they would never have it in this world, so their eye was set on the ultimate. They believed in making the best they could of life in this world while they were left in it because it was God's will, but they never expected much from this life and from this world. They knew it was a world of sin, a Vanity Fair, and so they passed through it as quickly as they could, as it were, untouched and untarnished by its tinsel and by all its sham and pretence. They went as pilgrims to America because they were already pilgrims in their minds and hearts and spirits. That seems to me to be the real ultimate explanation of these men. It was not merely their theological orthodoxy. What turned them into men of God was that they knew they were strangers and pilgrims in this evil world, journeymen on the way to God and to glory.

One other thing I would like to emphasize is this. What explains what happened to them? Here it seems to me that there is only one answer possible. It was *the providence of God* and his blessing upon them. We have been reminded that their original idea was to go to Virginia, but they soon had to abandon that. Then they thought to settle along the Hudson River, but they were not allowed to do so.

There is some dispute about the reason. Some say it was the treachery of the captain of the ship, although recently people have been trying to exonerate him. But whether it was that he was in league with the Dutch or not, and that they did not want them there, the fact is that they landed more in the neighbourhood of Cape Cod. The truth is that they never planned to go where they eventually landed.

I can draw no other conclusion from that amazing fact than that it was God who contrived this. Why? Well, for this reason: if they had landed near the Hudson River, as they intended, there is very little doubt but that every single one of them would have been killed. There were large numbers of vicious Indians there who killed many who landed in that particular area. God, I believe, did not allow them to land there. They had to go further north and eventually they landed in what we now know as Plymouth. And that was another most amazing providence. Did you know, I wonder, that only six months before they landed a pestilence had broken out amongst the Indians who lived in that area and, according to some authorities, nineteen-twentieths of the Indian population had been killed? So, six months before the pilgrims arrived, well ahead of time, nineteen-twentieths of the Indians who were to be their enemies had been removed out of the way. Is this accident? My dear friends, the story of the Pilgrim Fathers tells us not of the God of the deists but of the living God, who knows us one by one, who has counted the very hairs of our head and who watches over us and takes care of us in his fatherly and providential care.

Then another thing, which seems almost accidental, if you do not view things from the biblical standpoint, is that they were able to capture corn from some of the surviving Indians. That corn proved to be their salvation. It not only gave them food immediately, but it gave them seed for sowing later on in the year. Dr Woodbridge has reminded us that during that terrible winter half these people died of various illnesses. Do you know that even there one can see the providence of God? Because if those had not died, it is more than likely that, with the limited supply of food that they had, they would all have died of starvation. So God, as it were, mercifully took half away and left this remnant to carry on with the work.

But I have yet to tell you the most extraordinary thing of all. Two Indians appeared amongst them, quite unexpectedly. The Indians that remained had done their best to get rid of them. They had employed sorcerers to curse them and had invoked their devils, but all to no avail. Then two of them suddenly appeared amongst these settlers, welcoming them in broken English. Now how did this remarkable and providential happening in the life of these pilgrims come about?

One of these two Indians was named Squanto. My dear friends, I am telling you this that we may know that we have a living God, who sees the end from the beginning. Nothing happens by accident. Do you know the story of Squanto? It is this. Certain English adventurers landed from time to time in this very area. They went there to fish and for various other reasons. Unfortunately, they were bad and evil men and they would occasionally capture some of these Indians, take them on board their ships and use them as slaves. That is what happened to poor Squanto. He had become a slave to the English. Eventually they had sold him to someone in Spain but he managed to escape from there and make his way to England, where he lived for some time. It was while he was here that he picked up his little knowledge of English. And then, through the kindness of some men in this country he was able to go home and, believe it or not, this man Squanto arrived back in this very area six months before the arrival of the Pilgrim Fathers. He and his companion, as I say, visited the little settlement and were able to tell them about the number of the Indians and their attitude towards them, and were able to instruct them how to use the Indian corn. Everything that they needed most urgently these two men were able to provide for them.

So it all happened in that way. As God allowed Joseph to be wrongly taken captive and to go down into Egypt to prepare the way for the children of Israel in the famine, I believe he did precisely the same thing with Squanto in order to make it possible for the Pilgrim Fathers to settle in their plain. Indeed, subsequently, he was able to bring amongst them one of the greatest Indian chiefs in that whole area, and he made a treaty of peace with the Pilgrims and indeed became an English subject himself. I give you but these brief details in order that you may see that what ultimately accounts for the Pilgrim Fathers and all that their settlement there has led to during the intervening 350 years was not only their own sterling quality, their orthodox faith, their godliness and everything that I have emphasized concerning them, but it was ultimately the guiding hand of God. That is what emerges most clearly as you go through the history.

How are we to react?

Very well then, I shall try to sum up what we have been trying to say. How are we to react to all this? That is the big question. Surely none of us would be content with reacting merely in an antiquarian or merely historical manner. There are people who do that, you know — there are church historians and church historians. I have known church historians who could speak eloquently about the facts of the past but who in their own lives were utter contradictions of everything that they had been saying. Their interest was merely that of the historian or the antiquarian. I am sure that nobody here tonight is animated merely by such an antiquarian interest.

I also imagine that you will agree with me when I say that we must not react to this story in the way that Christopher Hill, the present Master of Balliol College, Oxford, does. I am going to quote you a sentence in his biography on Oliver Cromwell, entitled *God's Englishman*. From the purely historical standpoint this book has many things to commend it, until Mr Hill begins to give us his own theological opinions. This is one of them: he says, 'An approach to the world which in that period produced a Luther, a Milton and a Bunyan, will today produce nothing but psychiatric cases.' You see the idea, an approach to life which 350 and 400 years ago would produce a Luther or a Milton or a Bunyan will today produce nothing but a psychiatric case. In other words, his view is that if we are going to pay too much attention to the views of the Pilgrim Fathers on God, men and the purpose of existence, the result will be that we shall all become psychiatric cases. My only comment is this: would to God that England had more psychiatric cases! Is not this the very need? Look around at what happens when you reject these views! No, no, let us learn from the Pilgirim Fathers that this is the only true view of life. The opposite has been tried, and look at what it leads to! See the lawlessness among us — among students, in the homes, in industry, politically, everywhere. Lawlessness and confusion. This country may go down from industrial crises. Why? Because men no longer believe in God and are ready to bow before him. Every man is his own god; every man is as good as anybody else; every man's view is right. There was no king in Israel and every man did that which was right in his own sight. That is chaos, and we have it today. What is therefore needed is a return to the very views of life and this world which were held by these men.

So I say we do not react like Mr Christopher Hill. It is equally important that we do not react as our Lord says that the Pharisees and scribes behaved in his time and in his day. Listen to him in Matthew 23:29-32: 'Woe unto you, scribes and Pharisees, hypocrites! because ye build the tombs of the prophets, and garnish the sepulchres of the righteous, and say, If we had been in the days of our fathers, we would not have been partakers with them in the blood of the prophets. Wherefore ye be witnesses unto yourselves, that ye are the children of them which killed the prophets. Fill ye up then the measure of your fathers.'

Why do I say this? I say it because there are men, who have and are proposing to pay tribute to the Pilgrim Fathers, who deny their spirit and the practice. The ecumenical idea today is denying the spirit, the practice and the life of the Pilgrim Fathers and any tribute that they may attempt to pay to these men is hypocritical. These men stood for the great principles which we have been reminded of and if we do not stand for those principles we cannot honour them.

Very well, then, how do we honour them? I leave the answer in the form of a number of questions. *Do we hold the same doctrines as they held?* This is the first great question. Do we hold the same general doctrines about the Scriptures and their inerrancy? Do we hold the same view of the way of salvation as they held? But, more particularly, here is a question to evangelicals: are you subscribing to recent teaching, in the name of evangelicalism, which says that bishops are essential to the church, that they belong to the bone structure and skeleton of the Christian church? The Pilgrim Fathers did not and evangelicals, hitherto, have not done so either. Do we follow them in this that bishops are not essential to a new unified church? Do we agree with them in their view of sacramentalism and its practices? Are we equally clear in rejecting baptismal regeneration and various other sacramental errors? Do we agree with them in their view of the church of Rome, which to them was the great whore?

Now it is no use paying tribute to the Pilgrim Fathers unless you ask yourself these questions. Their views were quite unequivocal;

they were perfectly clear. I therefore ask, do we take these things seriously? These men took these things so seriously that they did what they did. Are these matters vital to us? Evangelical people, I am addressing you in particular, are you content to go on just as you are? Do you not think it is about time you faced these issues? These are not issues merely for preachers. They are issues for every member of the church.

So I go on to my next question: *are we ready to act on our beliefs as they were?* These men left the churches in which they had been brought up and nurtured. They left their homes; they left their relatives; they left their friends; they left their occupations; they even left their country! Eleven years in Holland and the rest in that wilderness in America! They faced the Atlantic, they faced the wilderness and all its horrors and possibilities and the antagonism of the Indians. They faced it all because of the principles which animated them.

But let me emphasize this as I close. History is vital, and exact history, precision, is important. 1620, remember, was in the age of James I. It was pre-Charles I. We know how things deteriorated sadly when Charles I came to the throne. But let me remind you that these men acted before Charles ever became king. Indeed, they also acted as they did in pre-Laudian days. You know how things deteriorated under Archbishop Laud. But these men acted before Laud ever became archbishop. These men separated in the pre-Charles, pre-Laudian days.

And let me remind you again, they were in general theological agreement with the others I have referred to. That was not the difference. The difference was over these matters of rites and ceremonies and church government. It was on those issues, in spite of the general theological agreement, they settled the question and faced the rigours of a cruel Atlantic and an unknown wilderness in the West. Now this is all I ask, if they were prepared to endure all that for those issues, if they were prepared to separate on those issues, are we not prepared to separate from those who are liberal in their doctrine, who deny the Christian faith, and who preach actively against it and ridicule it Sunday by Sunday from supposedly Christian pulpits? That is the challenge of the Pilgrim Fathers to us.

If they acted on their issues, how much more should we act on this issue of liberalism, a denial of the very elements of the Christian faith, and a rejection of the inerrancy and total authority of the

Scripture? Are we not also ready to divide on this issue of
sacramentalism, this issue of fraternizing with Rome? Indeed, is not
the call to us to separate from everything that is represented by the
World Council of Churches and the ecumenical movement? Are
you content to say, 'I do not want any trouble, I have always been
brought up in this chapel and I have always worshipped here'? There
are many evangelicals who are saying that to their pastors and
ministers today. They say, 'We agree about your theology but we do
not want to be disturbed. We have always done this.'

My dear friends, if you think like that and can sleep tonight after
hearing what you heard about the Pilgrim Fathers, I am in utter
despair with respect to you. You have no right to mention the
Pilgrim Fathers and pretend that you honour their memory. Face the
issues; face the facts. Or are you one of those who say, 'I am still
hopeful that I can reform the church in which I have been brought
up.' The answer of history to that is that the Pilgrim Fathers
anticipated by forty-two years the Great Ejection of 1662. It took the
rest forty-two years to see what these men had previously seen. By
1662 it was seen to be impossible and they took a stand which led
to their ejection from the Church of England. This is the testimony
of history. No, no! When a church is apostate or refuses repeated
attempts to discipline those in error on these matters, you cannot
reform her. This is the testimony of history. You must try to do so;
you must try to get discipline to be exercised. If they will not do so,
as Dr Woodbridge has reminded us, separate yourself from them
and 'be not partaker of their evil deeds'.

Have you heard the challenge of the Pilgrim Fathers? This is how
it comes to me:

A noble army, men and boys,
The matron and the maid
Around the Saviour's throne rejoice
In robes of light arrayed.
They climbed the steep ascent of heaven
Through peril, toil and pain.
O God, may grace to us be given
To follow in their train.

1. It does not appear from the section of Robinson's sermon found in Cotton Mather's *Magnalia Christi Americana* (vol. 1, p. 64) that he was thinking excusively of church government in the words quoted. Whether this is so or not, the famous sentence cannot be made to include the notions of modernism. To construe them in that way would be to make Robinson endorse the possibility that the opposite of his own views could arise from the Word of God. His express stipulation to test everything new by the Word is enough to dispose of such a fiction.

6.
Wrong divisions and true unity

The following address was given at Bethesda Chapel, Sunderland, on 4 November 1970. The Doctor had alluded to the message of 1 Corinthians on previous occasions, e. g., at Central Hall in 1966 and Liverpool in 1968. He now made extended use of it to demonstrate the difference between separation and schism. While repeating the need for the former, his main burden was that those who belonged to the BEC should not allow differences over matters which were not essential to the gospel to divide them. To do so would be schism.

It is a very great privilege that falls to me once more to give a closing word at an annual conference of the British Evangelical Council. It is also a very great pleasure because, as the chairman has just been saying, what this council stands for gives us hope for the future. To me, it is one of the most encouraging, if not the most encouraging, feature in evangelical life at the present time. Therefore, what little contribution I am enabled to make to it is made most gladly and with a great sense of privilege.

Now, I only wish that those who are here tonight and have not been in any previous meetings had been present earlier. We have had a very wonderful and encouraging day and particularly so, I feel, in the kind of meeting that we had together this afternoon when we listened to some brethren really giving us their experience. I venture to suggest to the authorities of this council that they should repeat that kind of meeting annually. I think we want to get back to an older conception of conference which is not merely one where things are theoretically discussed but where experiences are also shared. It is important to talk together as Christian people about the problems, the difficulties, the blessings and the glories of this Christian life.

It is never easy to know what the appropriate word is for an occasion like this because we are not only confronted by a complex general situation but also by a changing one. One therefore seeks for special and unusual guidance in the matter of a theme. And more and more, it seems to me, that the best thing I can do is to call your attention to the first four verses of the fifteenth chapter of Paul's first epistle to the Corinthians: 'Moreover, brethren, I declare unto you the gospel which I preached unto you, which also ye have received, and wherein ye stand; by which also ye are saved if ye keep in memory what I preached unto you, unless ye have believed in vain. For I delivered unto you first of all that which I also received, how that Christ died for our sins according to the Scriptures; and that he was buried, and that he rose again the third day according to the Scriptures.'

A day of confusion

There is no need for me to take any time in describing to you the age in which we live and the circumstances in which this conference is being held. We are living in a day which is characterized above everything else, it seems to me, by confusion. There are many other things that one could say about the present age, but if I were asked to choose one word which describes it I would have to choose the word 'confusion'.

I have been in the ministry and trying to preach now for getting on for forty-four years. I have seen strange things in the life of the churches, but I have never known such confusion as prevails at the present time. Of course, those of us who belong to this Evangelical Council are not a bit surprised that there is confusion among people who are not evangelical. They cannot but be confused. Indeed they are not evangelical because they are confused. So that does not surprise us. But, even in that realm, the confusion is more and more confounded than I have ever known it.

But what should be of particular concern to us is that we have to confess, if we are honest, that there is some confusion also even amongst us. This is serious. Of course, we are not foolish enough to imagine that one is ever in a perfect church here on earth. None of us would dare say that. We cannot do so in the light of Scripture. But we are entitled to expect a church which is at any rate free in general from this element of confusion. But we cannot say that such is the case. Now there is a sense in which this is not surprising. Great upheavals are taking place around us. Everything is being questioned and queried and all kinds of action are being taken. It is not surprising therefore that we should find ourselves a little confused at certain points and about certain matters. And it is to that that I want to address myself tonight.

What do we say about this, and what can we do about it? This is important because the greatest need in the world tonight is for a united evangelical message. It is the only hope for mankind. It is the only hope for the world and, in general, it is the only hope for the church. The people are confused, utterly confused. All their famous 'nostrums' fail to give them healing. All the prophecies of the false prophets have been falsified. They are all just disillusioned. That is the real meaning of this calamitous drug-taking and alcoholism. I believe the world is waiting for an authoritative statement. And it can only have it from those who take a scriptural view of the way of salvation — that is from evangelicals. That is why it is so urgently and vitally important that there should be no confusion amongst us but that we should speak with a united and a certain voice concerning these vital matters.

Lessons from 1 Corinthians

Well, now then, how do we approach our situation? I want to put it to you in this form. There are lessons which we urgently need to learn which are to be found in this first epistle to the Corinthians. I am more and more reminded today of the church at Corinth and I want to show you what a close parallel it presents to the situation that confronts us. The church at Corinth was a church that was full of troubles and confusion. This epistle we could describe as one of those 'omnibus' epistles which the apostle writes because he has to deal with a variety of different problems. He had received letters and spoken messages, as he tells us himself in the first chapter, from the house of Chloe and other people in Corinth, telling him about the troubles and the difficulties there. That is why he wrote his letter. He was not a literary man. He did not write for the sake of writing. He was too busy. He was a preacher and evangelist, a teacher and a traveller. Whenever he wrote he did so because he had to. There was never a church that was in need of such help and guidance as this tragically confused church at Corinth.

What has the apostle to say to them? Well, I think that my brethren will agree with me when I suggest that what he really says is that all their troubles were due to one fact. They had a defective and faulty view of the nature of the church. That was their basic trouble. I want to show you that as I go along. They were converted. They were born again. They were true Christians, but they were confused. Why? Because they were not clear in their understanding of the nature of the church. And how did that show itself? It did so, as you know, in the form of divisions, parties, schisms. That is what he keeps on saying to them.

But what were these divisions due to? What was the principle behind them? How did the church in Corinth, which was a very brilliant church in many ways — the apostle says that they were behind no other church in their dazzling gifts, and they were aware of that — how did they ever get into this confused condition with regard to the nature of the church?

I want to suggest to you that we can explain it in this form. All the divisions and the parties were due to the fact that they were standing and dividing on the wrong things. That leads us to a central theological question which I think is the essence of our problem at the present time. It is: 'What is the difference between schism and biblical separation?' I am going to illustrate this to you and show you the difference between them. Put in a practical manner, the question is, 'What are the things on which we should not take a stand? And what are the things on which we should take a stand?' Or if you like it in still a different way, 'What are the things that are not essential to our position? And on the other hand, what are the things that are essential to our position?' All the troubles in Corinth, and there were many, were due to their failure to draw the line properly between these various points. What do you stand on? What must you not stand on? On what grounds should you separate? On what ground should you not separate? What do you insist upon as being essential? What do you regard as being important but not essential? All their troubles were due to their failure to make that distinction.

Let me show you this. We will look first at the way in which the church in Corinth was standing and dividing on the wrong things and forming groups and parties on such matters. Those are the ones that the apostle takes up first. My understanding of this epistle is that the first fourteen chapters are devoted to an exposition by the apostle of the way in which the members of the church at Corinth were taking a stand on things which they should not have done. And then having dealt with these, patiently, as I read and understand him, he turns at the beginning of this fifteenth chapter from all those and in effect says, 'Now then, if you want to know what you should be standing on, here are those things. '

Wrong divisions in the church

But let us start with the negatives as he does. What were the wrong divisions in the church at Corinth? We can classify them under three headings. The first was *they were standing and dividing on carnal matters.* In their carnality they were quarrelling, forming parties and were rending the body of Christ. They were guilty of schism. This was the first thing. It was entirely carnal. What am I referring to? Well, the apostle puts it in his own language: 'It hath been declared unto me, my brethren, by them which are of the house of Chloe, that there are contentions among you.' Over what? 'Now this I say, that every one of you saith, I am of Paul; and I of Apollos; and I of Cephas; and I of Christ.' They were dividing and taking a stand on their favourite preachers, on their particular leaders. And they really had formed parties over this. They were not only contending, but they were actually forming parties and dividing. Now to divide over men is sheer carnality.

I need not take any time in applying these things. I am sure we are all perfectly clear about this. Alas! We have all known churches which have been formed solely on personalities. We have seen churches split and divided by difficult men, by arrogant men — men who want the pre-eminence. Is it not a tragic thing that people who are agreed about doctrine can divide and separate over personalities? They were guilty of that in Corinth. Let us examine ourselves. It has always seemed to me so unscriptural to name any church after a man. It has been equally wrong to give too much prominence to men. This happens not only amongst evangelicals but amongst others. You can go into a lot of churches and hear little about Jesus Christ but a lot about Barth and Bultmann. It is always men — men being preached, men being quoted, men being followed. Let us be careful that we never become guilty of a charge which I heard once brought against a youngish minister. A lady got up in a church meeting complaining that they had been hearing more about John Calvin than Jesus Christ from the pulpit in the last few months. My friends, we are not here to preach men or to stand for men. That is carnality. And the apostle deals with it as such and ridicules it as it deserves to be ridiculed.

But they were not only quarrelling among themselves but taking their quarrels, as he tells us in chapter 6, to the 'public law courts'. Christian people quarrelling before the world over matters that have nothing to do with the faith! And that was allowed to come in and to disturb the life of the church. This is sheer carnality. You remember that at the communion table, and even at the love feasts and so on, they were guilty of the same thing. Some people had too much food and some had too little. Some had been drinking too much, and some did not have enough to drink. And that was the cause of a division between the rich and the poor. So you see, some of the troubles were due to sheer carnality. Now the point is that people were taking a stand on these things. That is why I am putting this first as an illustration of taking a stand. They were refusing to yield over matters that are purely carnal.

But then there is a second category of things found in this epistle over which they were divided in the church. What was this? Well I would describe this as *'intellectualism'*. You notice that I say 'intellectualism'. There is nothing wrong with intellect, but intellectualism is an abomination. What am I referring to? Well, it is all here, as you know, in this epistle. People do not have an equal amount of brains and intellect. That is always the case. There is variety, as you know, with regard to this. That is why some of us have queries about the abolition of the eleven-plus examination. We are not all identical. Some are more knowledgeable than others. Now that was true in the church at Corinth, and instead of thanking God that some had greater understanding than others, this difference became a cause of division. The apostle has to take this up immediately in the first chapter. He is concerned that the philosophy which some were favouring would make the cross of Christ of none effect. Intellectualism can rob the gospel of its power.

Of course, those who were knowledgeable were very proud of themselves and tended to despise the others. He works that out in greater detail in chapter 8 with regard to the different views taken concerning the matter of meat offered to idols. Now, you see, when these people had been pagans they took their meat to the temples as offerings to the gods. Having done so, they regarded them as sacred and believed it was wrong to eat them. But, having become Christians, what were they to think? They did not all immediately see the truth in exactly the same way on this matter. The more intelligent people, the more enlightened people could see at a glance that there was nothing wrong in eating the food. Why? Because they knew that idols do not actually exist. They are only figments of the imagination. Therefore there was nothing wrong with the food which had been offered to them. But there were other brethren, weaker brethren, who still felt it was wrong to eat these meats. This was actually dividing the church at Corinth. The more intellectual people were despising the rest and they were offended at the intellectuals. The whole church was in this tragic condition of schism — over intellectual understanding.

Now you say, 'What has that to do with us?' My dear friends, I am afraid it has a great deal to do with us, as it has often had a great deal to do with the life of the church throughout the centuries. There is always a danger of a kind of scholasticism among evangelical people. What I mean is that it is the people who are interested in doctrine and the importance of intellectual apprehension and understanding who tend to despise those who are less capable than they are in that respect. They say of their brethren, 'They know no doctrine.' They despise them. There are groups and divisions which are based solely, not upon their common experience of regeneration, but upon the amount of intellect they happen to have and their intellectual comprehension and understanding. Instead of joining together to thank God for varying gifts in this respect as in others, they tend to rend the church. And you get factions and divisions, with jealousy and envy on the one hand and a spirit of superiority and of despising the less learned on the other. That was one of the great causes of division and schism in the church at Corinth. They were standing on intellect and intellectual apprehension and making this central.

And thirdly, there was division and schism owing to what I am compelled to describe as *'false spirituality'*. I am referring of course to chapters 12, 13 and 14, where the apostle at the beginning of chapter 12 says, 'Now concerning spirituals...' He means, 'concerning spiritual gifts', and goes on in these three most important chapters to show how the church in Corinth was actually divided into groups and factions and the body of Christ was, as it were, being rent over spiritual gifts. He puts it before us in detail. He shows how ridiculous this whole attitude is, by saying such things as, 'The body is not one member, but many. If the foot shall say, Because I am not of the hand, I am not of the body; is it therefore not of the body? And if the ear shall say, Because I am not the eye, I am not of the body; is it therefore not of the body?' What a tragic state of affairs! Instead of rejoicing together in the gifts that God had given to them as a church they had made the gifts themselves into a cause of division. Why? Well, because some were standing on this gift, and others on some other gift.

It is clear that the main stand was being taken over the question of speaking in tongues and that this was what was being put at the centre. There were those who were saying that if you did not have this gift it was doubtful whether you were a Christian at all. But, even short of that, there were those who were claiming to be superior Christians because they had this or some other gift and tended to despise those who had lesser gifts. And the poor people who had 'lesser gifts', that is, those which were regarded as lesser by carnal Christians, were envious and jealous of those people who had the more spectacular gifts.

My dear friends, is this ancient history? Has this nothing to say to us? Is there not even a danger today that some people take a stand on this matter and make it central, indeed crucial? Now, that was the third great cause of trouble in the church at Corinth, and it is in that context the apostle uses the term 'schism', charging them with its guilt. They had forgotten that the church was the body of Christ and that they were all particular members of it. They were guilty of schism.

You see how all these things are just illustrations of the way in which the members of the church at Corinth were failing to draw the distinction between the things on which a stand should or should not be taken. They were taking up this attitude: 'It must be Paul'; 'It must be Apollos'; 'You must have this intellect'; 'You must speak in tongues'; 'You must have this or that gift.' Now there, you see, are the great instances in this mighty epistle of men and women dividing when they should not divide, separating when they should not, regarding as essential what is not essential and so dividing the body of Christ. The apostle has taken them through all this. He has had to. It has been wearisome but necessary because these things were causing such trouble in the church. 'Oh', says Paul, 'what a tragedy it is that you are taking your stand on these carnal matters, on an intellectualism and on this false notion of spirituality!' 'Listen', he says in chapter 15, 'I will tell you what you should be taking your stand on.' I never read this chapter without detecting a note of impatience in it. Because all the while that they had been standing on the wrong things, they had been neglecting the right ones. What were these right things?

My dear friends, it is my privilege to remind you of these. I am not surprised that the masses of the people are outside the Christian church in this country today. How can they have a true impression of Christianity in the light of what they see on the television, hear on the radio and read in their newspapers? How can you expect them to know what the Christian faith is? And if you and I do not unite in telling them this, but spend our time in standing on things which we should not, they will remain in the darkness and ignorance of sin.

Things on which we must stand

Now, says Paul, there are some things on which we have got to stand. These are the things that we must regard as essential and over which we must be prepared to separate. He makes this clear by saying, 'Moreover, brethren, I declare unto you the gospel which I preached unto you, which also ye have received, and wherein ye stand.' This is the place to stand. What are these things? Well, let me just note them for you because I believe we ought to remind ourselves of these things at least once a year. We cannot take them for granted, lest they go by default.

The Scriptures

What is the first thing we stand on? You notice that he refers to the Scriptures. 'I delivered unto you first of all that which I also received, how that Christ died for our sins *according to the Scriptures.*' Why did he add that? Why did he not just say, 'I delivered unto you first of all that which I also received, how that Christ died for our sins'? Why does he add, 'according to the Scriptures'? And then again: 'that he was buried, and that he rose again the third day *according to the Scriptures*'? Why include this? Why waste ink and breath? Well, because this is crucial and fundamental. If we are not clear about our stand on the Scriptures, then our whole position is not only shaken, it has collapsed.

What does he mean by 'the Scriptures'? Well, fortunately he tells us in these four verses. What is our view of the Scriptures? By the way, let me remind you that we take our entire stand on the Scriptures, not on tradition in any shape or form, neither as taught by the Roman Catholics nor in the more subtle use of the term by pseudo-Catholics. What is our stand on the Scriptures? Well, here it is in one word — revelation! We stand on the Scriptures because we say that these Scriptures are given by way of revelation.

You notice how he puts it: 'I delivered unto you first of all that which I also received.' How often does he say this? You see, here is the great dividing line. Here is the tendency that began in the last century and even before then, the so-called 'higher criticism'. What is the basis of that? Well its basis is that you depend upon philosophy; you do not submit as a little child to the Scriptures, but you talk about seeking and searching after truth. You engage in a great quest and enquiry because you say you cannot expect twentieth-century people to believe what was believed in the past because of the new knowledge which has been acquired. Now here is the great fight which has to be fought all over again. We do not base our position on philosophy, on searching or on investigation.

Indeed, the whole story of Paul makes it impossible for him ever to have occupied such a position. How did that man who preached the gospel to them in Corinth ever become a Christian? Was it as the result of his study and investigation, his research and his enquiry? We know the answer, do we not? He had to be knocked down. Paul did not become a Christian at the end of a process of reason and of logic. It was quite the reverse. He had to be smitten, to be struck. He had to see the risen Lord. *Revelation!* And he goes on saying, not only here but everywhere, that what he delivered to them was what he received. Listen to how he puts it to the Galatians. He says, 'I never received it of men nor was I taught it, but by the revelation of God.' Now this is our basic position. We are not interested in the latest research or the latest results of investigation. We are not interested in the speculations of the twentieth century. We say that what we have is what has been revealed and we know nothing saving apart from this.

Then the element of *inspiration* comes in. He had already said in the second chapter that they declare the things that have been revealed in 'words that the Spirit giveth'. It is not only the general ideas which were given by God the Holy Spirit, but also the very words in which they were expressed. That is our view of Scriptures. 'All Scripture is given by inspiration of God.' It is God-breathed. 'No prophecy of Scripture comes by private interpretation. Holy men of God spoke as they were moved by the Holy Ghost.' These were not religious seers. It was not man thinking or enquiring. Men were given the revelation and even the words in which to write it down and express it. This is our view of Scripture. It is entirely given and we take our stand on this. There should be no modification. We do not add anything to it. We do not say that we can read things behind, and not in, the words of Scripture because of the light which later history and the church has thrown on them. We reject that we are now able to know things which the early Christians did not know. The Scripture comes to us as it came to the first Christians. And we receive it as the apostles, the writers themselves, had received it.

But remember there is a conclusion which we draw from this. Because the Scriptures are 'revelation' and 'inspiration', they are *authoritative*. They are ageless, changeless, because they are God's revealed truth which he enabled men to record. As a result, the passing of the centuries does not make the slightest difference to them. Further, we do not admit that the fact that we are living in the twentieth century makes the slightest difference to us in our attitude to the Scriptures. It is the truth given once and for ever. So we accept that the Scripture is as authoritative as it was in the first century and as it will be if there shall be future centuries. It it final because it is of God.

But I must add another thing and this is something new *for us* to say as evangelicals. We not only must say that we accept the Scriptures. We have got to accept the whole of Scripture — the entire Scriptures, the Old Testament as well as the New, because it is all the Word of God. Let me put this point in another way. We have to accept the history of the Bible as well as its doctrine. You know, there is a new teaching that is being presented by some evangelicals who tell us that the Scriptures are only concerned about religious truth. They say, 'We accept the supreme authority of the Scriptures, but, of course' — they carry on to add — 'the Scriptures are only concerned to give us religious truth. They are only to give us truth concerning salvation. We do not come to the Scriptures to find out how the world was created. That is science.' Are you aware of these subtle changes, my friends? There is a new teaching which tells us that we take the Scriptures as fully authoritative in matters of salvation, in the nurture of the soul and moral conduct, but in nothing else. Consequently, when we want our knowledge about other things we go to nature and we listen to the modern scientist. This is serious because it means rejecting the historical portions of Scripture and the scriptural account of the creation of the world.

I can show you, from this fifteenth chapter of Paul's first epistle tto the Cortinthans, that to say this is to deny the authority of Scriptures. The apostle here, you notice, talks about Adam. Now there are evangelicals who do not believe in Adam as a single individual and as the first man. They say that Genesis is poetry, symbolism. It is myth. But you notice that the apostle rests his whole case upon history as well as on doctrinal teaching. Notice how he keeps on bringing in Adam: 'As in Adam all die...' He, and the Lord Jesus Christ before him, believed the account in Genesis of the origin and creation of the world and of the first man, Adam. And I assert that to make the distinction which we are referring to is a departure from evangelicalism — a departure that will deprive us of all our authority and begin among us a slide into liberalism and even to Roman Catholicism. We must not let go of this vital principle. We must believe the whole Bible, its history as well as its teaching about salvation; its account of creation as well as its account of the new creation and the final glorification. That is the thing which the apostle puts first in his list of essentials — the Scriptures: 'according to the Scriptures'.

The Fall

The second great note he sounds is that, as evangelicals, we always have to emphasize the doctrine of the Fall and the need of salvation. 'Moreover, brethren, I declare unto you the gospel which I preached unto you, which ye also have received and wherein ye stand, by which also ye are saved.'

Do we need to be saved? There are people who say that we do not. But the Bible teaches that we do. Why do we need to be saved? Why did the Son of God ever have to come into this world? Do you know the answer? 'As in Adam all men died...' Adam — history again you see — 'according to the Scriptures'. You have no gospel if you deny history. The whole argument depends on this parallel of what happened in Adam and what happened in Christ, on the contrast between them as well as on the similarity.

The world does not believe this. I saw a discussion on the television which dealt with the following question: 'Why is there suffering in the world?' No one referred to the Fall. They had no explanation of suffering and evil and that is why they have got no saving message.

Why is the world as it is today? There is only one answer. It is God's world. He made it absolutely perfect. He looked at it and saw that it was good. It is not a failure in evolution which has caused the current problems. God made the world, put a perfect man in it and he looked at him and all the creation and saw that it was all good. Why, then, is the world as it is today? Because man listened to the tempter, defied God and rebelled against him, spat in his face and went his own way — the fall of man in Adam! And we have no message for the modern world if we do not preach this: Adam, historicity, creation and Fall, 'according to the Scriptures'.

And you notice how the epistle goes on to tell us that there are other notes which we must emphasize. There is God's wrath against sin. Did you notice these words? 'If Christ be not risen, then is our preaching vain, and your faith is also vain. Yea, ... we are also found false witnesses ... for if the dead rise not, then is not Christ raised: and if Christ be not raised, your faith is vain; you are yet in your sins. Then they also which are fallen asleep in Christ are perished. If in this life only we have hope in Christ, we are of all men most miserable.' My dear friends, who is there in the world to preach the wrath of God against sin and judgement, perdition and perishing, unless we do so? This is apostolic preaching.

Now I want to emphasize this to you. The apostle says that these are the things which he preached first of all to them. There is a debate among the learned commentators as to the meaning of 'first of all'. Is it first chronologically or first in importance? I believe it is both. He put first the things which should come first. It is the most

important things with which one begins. You see, these foolish
Corinthians had been arguing about men and gifts and this and that,
and so on. And Paul says, 'Look here, the things that come first are
these.' And if you and I do not put these things first, we are ceasing
to be evangelicals. So you see, we have got to put first the fall of man,
man in sin, man under the wrath of God, man facing perdition, man
perishing if he dies in his sins. This is an essential part of our
preaching, the Fall and its consequences. It is we alone, as evangelicals, who believe this truth and who therefore must preach it.

God's plan of redemption

But I must hurry on. He then unfolds to them God's great plan of
redemption. And here, of course, is his main reason for bringing in
this phrase, 'according to the Scriptures': 'I delivered unto you first
of all that which I also received, how that Christ died for our sins
according to the Scriptures'. What does that mean? Well, what he
means is this. Here is our troubled world in its agony and pain. Is
there any hope, any message for it? Thank God there is! That is what
we are here for. But what is it? It is that in spite of everything that
is true today, this is still God's world and he has not abandoned it.
I can go further. He formed a plan for the redemption of this world
even before he created it. The apostle Paul says that. Listen to him:
'We speak the wisdom of God in a mystery, even the hidden wisdom
which God ordained before the world unto our glory.' 'According
to the Scriptures' — it is not an after-thought. This is the essential
message of the whole Bible. God's plan of redemption for this whole
cosmos is according to what he has revealed in the Scriptures.

Where did he reveal it in the Scriptures? Well, you have got to
go back to history again. Where is the first promise of redemption
in the Scriptures? I must tell you that it is in the third chapter of
Genesis, and it was made to a man called Adam and his wife's name
was Eve. 'According to the Scriptures', the man and the woman
sinned and, being conscious of it and ashamed, they went and hid
themselves behind the trees. But God, in his infinite grace, came
down and walked in the garden in the cool of the evening. And he
called to him, 'Adam, where art thou?' And the poor fool had to
come out in his sin and shame. God then told him the consequences
of his utter folly and of the suffering that was to follow, which has

followed us to this very night. You have got lawlessness in this country tonight because of the fall of Adam. It is in all of us. We are born in sin. We are shapen in iniquity. You have no explanation of the industrial strife, of the way in which men belonging to trades unions will not obey their own leaders, and why children will not obey their parents, except the fall of Adam. And it has been going on ever since.

But, thank God, he looked at Adam and Eve, even in their condemnation and sin and shame, and he gave them the first promise of redemption. He said that there would be enmity between the seed of the serpent and the seed of the woman. In the conflict between them, the woman's seed would bruise the head of the serpent, but only his heel would be bruised. Christ is going to be wounded, but Satan is going to be destroyed. You see, 'Christ died for our sins according to the Scriptures.' The old scriptural account of what God said when he came down into the Garden of Eden and told them that by the seed of the woman, (note, without the man, i. e. virgin birth) redemption was going to come to the human race is vital. That is why Paul says, 'according to the Scriptures'. If you reject and jettison Adam and Eve and the historicity of the Fall, if you reject a belief in the factual history as well as the didactic portions of Scripture, you will ultimately have no biblical doctrine of redemption whatsoever. It is the key to an understanding of Romans 5 as well as to this great chapter of First Corinthians.

Now I could take you through the whole of the Old Testament. What would I be showing you? How that Christ was to die according to the Scriptures. Cain and Abel — why was one offering better than another? Why all this business in the book of Leviticus — all this about burnt offerings and sacrifices? I know superficial evangelical Christians who do not bother to read that sort of thing. They say, 'It has nothing to do with us.' Has it not? Christ died for our sins, my friend, according to the Scriptures. It was God who ordered all that, who ordained it and commanded it. And why? Because he was giving a promise to the people. These are all adumbrations, foreshadowings of the one perfect offering that was to come. If you do not delight in Leviticus — I must be careful that I do not fall into the error of the intellectuals in Corinth — but do you see, my friends, the importance of taking all the Scriptures? All the burnt offerings, all the sacrifices, all the shadows and types — what do they mean?

Well, Paul puts it in the second epistle to these Corinthians: 'All the promises of God in him are yea and in him, Amen.' They are all pointing to him, every one of them and in every detail, and he has fulfilled them every one. Everything he has done is according to the Scriptures.

The person of the Lord

But now we come to our great central truth about the person of the Lord, the babe of Bethlehem, the carpenter, the young man who began to preach at the age of thirty. Who is he? John the Baptist answered that question when he pointed two of his disciples to him and said, 'Behold, that is the Lamb of God that taketh away the sin of the world.' Not the lambs daily provided by men; not the blood of bulls and of goats and the ashes of an heifer, but God's own Lamb. He said, 'There he is — the Lamb of God that taketh away the sin of the world.' Who is this Jesus? Paul, you see, makes this central. This is what they all preached — Jesus and the resurrection. 'Born of the seed of David according to the flesh, but declared to be the Son of God with power according to the Spirit of holiness by the resurrection from the dead.' Who is this? And the apostle answers his own question by saying, 'The first man is of the earth, earthy. The second man is the Lord from heaven.' Basic, absolutely basic and central, is it not? This is what we are here to assert and to preach.

And then, let me emphasize something else, which is more needed perhaps at this present time than it has been for many a long day. What did the apostle preach about this blessed person Jesus, the Son of God? What did he tell them in Corinth about him? Was it his teaching? Was it his example? Was it his death as a pacifist? Do you notice what he says? Does he say, 'I delivered unto you first of all that which I received, how that Christ lived a perfect life, gave the Sermon on the Mount, gave us this wonderful example and illustration of what to do and how to live, and all we have got to do is to rise up and follow him and imitate him' — as if we could thereby save ourselves? No, no! What he says is extraordinary. His life and teaching are important and that is why we have the four Gospels. But Paul says that when he preached to them the saving gospel, what was central in it was that *'Christ died for our sins'*. He went straight from Christ's birth to his death. Why? Because this is what saves us, not the teaching or the example. There would be no salvation apart from this. He singles out the death, the burial and the glorious resurrection.

And, remember, my friends, the whole point of 1 Corinthians 15 is to tell us that *the resurrection was a physical and historical event.* This is a very physical chapter. He did not teach them that the influence of Christ remained or resurfaced in their minds. No, no! He teaches the literal, physical resurrection of the body. And he must do so, because if the body is not going to be saved then the devil has had the victory. Man was made body, soul and spirit and was perfect. When man fell, he fell in this threefold respect. I am not merely formed in a spiritual sense; my body is also formed. It is the body of my humiliation. And if my body is not going to be redeemed and restored then the devil has the final victory. No, no! The apostle preaches the literal, physical resurrection, and we are here to preach it, though we do not understand it. It was a fact. He was seen. There were witnesses and he gives you the details. Why does he trouble to do so unless the physical element is central and all-important?

'Well,' says the apostle, 'this is what I preached to you.' These were the first things, the centralities. To the Galatians he wrote, 'I placard Christ crucified to you.' He was like a man going around putting up posters, placarding Christ dying for our sins, being buried, rising again, 'for our sins'. Remember *substitutionary atonement.* That is the evangelical position. This 'for' marks the penal substitution. 'He bore my sins in his own body on the tree.' 'God has laid on him the iniquity of us all.' Isaiah said that in the Scriptures and it has happened. 'He has made him to be sin for us, who knew no sin; that we might be made the righteousness of God in him.' The apostle had preached to them these great facts of the complete message based upon the ancient history. He not only stated the facts, but he gave them the meaning. That is essentially evangelical preaching.

But we must not leave it at that, must we? Remember the ultimate thing that the apostle reminds us of in this very chapter. What we preach is indeed the truth of God. But we do not stop merely at personal salvation and deliverance from the power and guilt of sin while we are in this world. We also preach sanctification — a gradual deliverance from the pollution of sin. But we go even beyond that. We look forward to *a blessed hope.* Listen to him putting it here in this grand climax: 'He must reign, till he hath put all enemies under his feet. The last enemy that shall be destroyed is death. For he hath put all things under his feet. But when he saith, all things are put under him, it is manifest that he is excepted, which did put all things under him. And when all things shall be subdued unto him, then shall the Son also himself be subject unto him that put all things under him, that God may be all in all.' The only hope for this wretched old world tonight is that the Son of God is going to come back to it, riding the clouds of heaven, surrounded by the holy angels, and he will come to judge. He is the judge of the whole cosmos and he will adjudicate and destroy all his enemies, the devil and his followers, and all men and women who have listened to the devil and who have died in their sins. They will go to perdition. Then he will purge the entire cosmos from every relic and remnant of sin and will return to his Father a restored and a perfected universe and God shall be all in all. Our redemption, the redemption that we preach, is not only individual and personal. Thank God, it is also a cosmic redemption and every trace of sin and its influence will be banished and destroyed to all eternity.

Now, says the apostle, those are the things on which you must stand, and which you must never compromise. Consequently, they are the things on which you separate from all who do not accept them. How do you do so? Well, I have not time to tell you, but one of the important things is this: 'Be not deceived. Evil communications corrupt good manners.' If you keep bad company, you will become bad yourself. And that, let me remind you, refers not only to conduct and behaviour, but still more so to belief. If it is a dangerous thing to mix with people who live evil lives, who say, 'Let us eat, drink and be merry, for tomorrow we die,' if that is dangerous, how much more dangerous is it to mix with people who deny the vital essential elements of this truth!

Look at the attention which is being paid today to the problem of pollution of the atmosphere, of the sea, of the rivers. Quite right! But I will tell you something that is infinitely more dangerous. It is pollution of the mind, pollution of the soul and of the spirit. And if you mix with polluted doctrine it is not surprising that you become diseased and more or less useless in the kingdom of God. 'Evil communications corrupt good manners.' Take your stand, says Paul. How do you take your stand? Well, you avoid evil communications.

You have nothing to do with them. You do not bid Godspeed to, or welcome into your house, a man who denies this essential truth.

What else do you do? Well, he tells us in the next chapter to 'stand fast in the faith. Watch ye.' What, my dear friends, are you watching? Are you aware of the subtle influences that are coming in? They are speaking to you on the television. I remember a few years back talking to some evangelical people who had seen the late Pope John XXIII on the television. And this is what they said: they were impressed by the fact that he looked a very nice old man. And I think they were beginning to doubt, you know, whether his doctrines were wrong because he looked so nice. Watch ye, my dear friends. Watch! Our Lord left this command. The apostle repeats it: 'Watch ye. Stand fast in the faith.' Do not yield at any point. Stand fast in the faith. Quit you like men. Be strong. You will need it. You will be persecuted, laughed at, derided, attacked in subtle ways. Be strong, quit you like men. Go forward void of fear.

Now these are the things on whch we stand as evangelical people and I, for one, am content with the apostle Paul's list. This is his list, not mine. I notice that the lists of men are generally longer than the lists of the apostles. Beware, my friends, beware, lest you add so much that you cause division. These are the 'first of all' things, says Paul, the things of primary importance. These are the things that you must stand on.

Differences among evangelicals

But then, you say, what about the things on which we differ as evangelicals? What about them? I can give you the answer which the apostle gives. It is in chapter 8. Let me read it to you first and then expound it to you. This is how he puts it: 'Wherefore, if meat make my brother to offend, I will eat no flesh while the world standeth, lest I make my brother to offend.' Listen again, 'Through thy knowledge shall the weak brother perish, for whom Christ died?' There are some men who do not take the same view as you do of a particular doctrine. What are you going to do? Well, I will tell you what I am going to do. If I am convinced that that man is my brother I am going to bear with him. I am not going to divide from him. What makes us one is that we are born of the same blood, of the same Spirit. We are born again by the same Spirit into the same family. Such a man is my

brother. I am not going to divide from him because I believe his
intellect is inferior to mine. Thank God, I think I am enough of a
Christian to say this, that if I do think he is intellectually inferior, I
am prepared not only to bear with him patiently, but to give him
more time than I give to the man who has got more intellect than I
have. If there is a brother in your family who is slow of understanding, do you throw him out? Do you refuse to speak to him? Do you
refuse to co-operate with him? Of course you do not. Evangelical
people, brotherhood comes first! It takes precedence over intellectual understanding. It was because they missed that that they
were dividing wrongly in Corinth. If this man is my brother, for
whom Christ died, if he is as born again as I am, I refuse to separate
from him. I may think he is very mistaken. I have often thought so,
and we often think so about one another, but I am not going to
separate from him. I am not going to divide from him or dismiss him.
If he has less knowledge than I have, I ought to try to teach him and
to educate him. Why, he is my brother. For the man who is not my
brother, I have no hope until he is born again. I have only one thing
to preach to him. It is that he is a sinner under the wrath of God and
that unless he repents he goes to perdition. But I do not separate from
my brother. There is my first canon.

My second principle is the one that the apostle puts next. People
say to me that they hold their views on conscientious grounds. 'I
must obey my conscience,' they say. 'You must not ask me to
tolerate these views which do not agree with mine, perhaps on
prophecy, or baptism, or on holiness, or on any one of these matters.
This is matter of conscience to me.' Is that what you are saying?
Then you are a Corinthian. That is exactly what they were saying in
the church at Corinth: 'my conscience'. Remember that Paul says to
them, 'conscience not thine own, but of the other also'!

Paul says, 'I have got a right to eat this meat. I am sufficiently
enlightened to see this, but if meat make my brother to offend, I will
eat no flesh while the world standeth, lest I make my brother to
offend.'

My dear, good, evangelical friends, I have been contending for
most of my ministerial life for the importance of doctrine and
understanding. But if you are going to make your understanding of
doctrine a cause of offence to your weaker brother for whom Christ
died, if you are putting your conscience first and never considering
his conscience at all, then you are being utterly unscriptural,

unspiritual and unchristian. Let us be careful, brethren. The tests that we put at the centre are those of our blessed relationship to our Lord. We are brothers. Families are strange mixtures, but we are a family, the family of God. We are different, yes, but we are all brethren. We have got the same life in us; we are all partakers of the divine nature. We have been born from above, born of the Spirit. We are one; we are all going to heaven. Well, let us march there together and bear one another's burdens and so fulfil the law of Christ. 'Conscience, not thine own, but of the other also.'

In other words, put into the centre the things that the apostle puts into the centre. Stand on those unflinchingly, without the slightest suspicion of accommodation or modification. Stand on them even unto death, but be very careful about anything else you stand on, lest you become guilty of the sin of schism and offend a dear brother for whom Christ died. If you think he is mistaken, patiently, quietly, prayerfully, try to instruct him and to help him. And as you value your own conscience and always try to obey it, remember that he has got a conscience also and you must not cause him to offend it. Let us love one another. Let us bear with one another but hold the centralities, the first things, boldly, courageously and unflinchingly together.

Well, my dear friends, there, it seems to me, is the apostle's order of the day for us. We have separated, most of us, from what we must. But God forbid that we should stand over against or divide and separate brethren who together with us are those for whom Christ died, and who therefore look forward to sharing the glory of eternity together.

7.
The state of the nation

This address was delivered at Westminster Chapel on 3 November 1971 and was published in booklet form in the following year. It is an example of the Doctor's ability to diagnose and to prescribe — in moral and spiritual terms. The alarming features of contemporary life are documented, together with the church's part in them, before the only adequate repsonse for individual Christians and the church is described. The gospel — and revival — provide the only answer. The members of the large congregation were sobered and greatly encouraged by the address.

No subject at the present time calls for more serious and urgent attention than the state of the nation. Almost daily one finds in articles and letters in the more serious daily papers, and in discussions on the television and radio, an increasing concern about the state of affairs as we see them, and know them, and experience them at the present time. We are in a very serious predicament.

Some of the greatest leaders in the various branches of thought are giving expression to this in very striking terms. Professor Arnold Toynbee, in his latest book called *Surviving the future*, uses these words: 'The morality gap is greater than ever before.' Now this comes from the man famous for his massive *Study of History* in ten volumes, and who has spent his life in studying and trying to understand the movements of history throughout the centuries in every country. That is the conclusion at which he arrives, that the morality gap is greater than ever before. He goes on to say, 'The world is being dehumanized.'

Let me quote another — Professor Sir John Eccles, an Australian, possibly the greatest neuro-scientist or brain scientist in the world today and a Nobel Prize winner. As the result of his scientific studies for a number of years he, again in a recent book called *Facing Reality* says, 'In this tragic hour we must know what we are fighting for; we must appreciate man's greatness; we must regain our faith and hope in man and his destiny, else all is lost.'

In those quotations from two great humanists we have a perfect description of our present position and predicament.

I do not propose to indulge in a lurid description of the moral state of degradation of this country today. I have not seen *Oh! Calcutta*, neither have I been to Denmark recently! So I am not going to entertain you with a description of the excesses and perversions that are to be seen on the stage at the present time. Neither am I going to bore you with quotations from contemporary literature illustrative of the prurience and the pornography of which we hear so much at the present time. All this is well known to us and, in any case, there is a sense in which all that is but one manifestation of our real problem and predicament. The problem itself is much greater, deeper, much more serious.

A historical perspective

As we approach this subject it is most important that we should realize that this is not the first time that this country, or the world, has been in its present condition. One great advantage of knowing the Bible and its message is that one gets a right perspective on history. One discovers that there have been similar periods before, and secular history shows that there have been similar periods subsequent to biblical history. We think of the Restoration period and of the period of the Regency, and others. There is a sense, therefore, in which what we are facing today is not new; and yet there is another sense in which, as I hope to show, there is a new element.

There have often been periods of gross sinfulness, moral degradation, riotous living, and so on; but there is an additional factor today, and it is this which I regard as being most desperately serious. We are not merely faced with disobedience today; we are faced with a denial of all moral principles and of even the very concept of law itself. The position is put perfectly in the third verse of the eleventh Psalm: 'If the foundations be destroyed, what can the righteous do?' That, surely, is the position at the present time.

I have sometimes ventured on a medical analogy to try to show what in my opinion is the great difference, say, between conditions today and what they were at the beginning of the eighteenth century before the great Evangelical or Methodist Awakening. The conditions that prevailed in the early part of the eighteenth century are well known; we have had many eloquent descriptions of them, including that found in the biography of George Whitefield by Dallimore. They were desperate; it was the 'gin' age, and immorality and vice were rampant.

What is the difference between that age and the present age? My illustration puts it like this. Imagine that you were walking along a road and that suddenly you see a man lying at the side of a hedge. It has been raining heavily, and you feel that this is dangerous for the man's health. So you go to him and take hold of him and shout at him and perhaps shake him in order to awaken him. Now that man may be in one of two conditions. It may be that he was just very tired after walking a great distance, and fatigue had overcome him; so he had put himself down to have a rest, and had fallen asleep. He was so soundly asleep that he did not know that it had been raining; so you shout at him and shake him and rouse him, and he is grateful to you and continues on his journey.

But there is another possibility. It may be that that man is in that condition because he has taken some drug — it may be an excess of alcohol, or some other drug. In other words, he has a poison in his system. Now if it is the second condition all the shouting in the world is not going to help him. You can shake him and shout at him, until you are exhausted; but you will not help him. In this second condition you have to get rid of the poison which is causing the unconsciousness.

That analogy should help us to understand the point I am making about a new factor. The position at the beginning of the eighteenth century, more or less, was that people were just disobedient. They did not deny the reality of the supernatural realm. The masses did not deny the being of God. They were just lazy, forgetful, indeed asleep. What they needed was the rousing awakening ministry of Whitefield, the Wesleys and others to awaken them, to shake them out of their lethargy and to show them their danger. But that is no longer the position. A poison has been introduced into the intellectual, moral and religious systems; a teaching has permeated the thinking of the nation which is polluting and drugging it, so that today a mere attempt at awakening the people is totally insufficient. We have to get rid of the poison before there can be any hope.

The role of the church

It is at this point that we can ask the question: 'What, then, can be done in the present position?' I am not merely referring to the permissiveness and the pornography, but also to the industrial unrest, to the attitude of mind which has become increasingly cynical and to the lawlessness which is evident in all classes of society and in almost every walk of life.

What has the Christian church to say to all this? I would start by laying down three principles, which I deem to be very important. The first is that *the state of the church has generally determined the state of the nation.* I could easily demonstrate that from history were time to permit. It is surely obvious that the greatest periods in the history of this land have always been the periods that have followed religious revival and reawakening. I am thinking of the Elizabethan period, the Commonwealth and the Victorian era.

The second principle is that *the relationship between the state of the church and the state of the nation is an indirect one,* not direct. There is great confusion about this but, to me, it is essential that we should realize that the influence of the church upon the state is an indirect one, not a direct one.

The third principle which I hope to demonstrate is that the difference between the church's view of the present situation and all other views, is that *it is the church alone which has a profound, and not a superficial, understanding of the problem which confronts us, and also the only remedy that avails.* The church is not concerned, as so many others, simply to 'describe' the situation. That can be done so easily, and it is quite a popular occupation at the present time. But it is too superficial. We cannot afford merely to describe the position; our business is to try to understand it. By the church I mean those who still believe the Bible to be the Word of God, and whose thinking is governed by it.

The cause of the nation's condition

We must start by trying to discover the cause of this present condition of society which we all bemoan. Here it is important to realize that this has not come about suddenly. It did not arise with the performance of *Oh! Calcutta* or *Hair*. This has been a very long story. We are witnessing today the end of a process which has been going on for at least two centuries, perhaps even longer.

What accounts for the present state of affairs? I can divide my answer under two main headings: there are certain general causes; then there is what we can describe as *the* cause.

General causes

By general causes I mean that certain things have happened in thought and practice which have tended to produce the present serious condition. What are they? We can at any rate trace it back to the end of the last century when an obvious reaction began to set in against Victorianism. It was a reaction against the pomposity of Victorianism, its smug self-satisfaction and its hypocrisy. I am as much a critic of Victorianism as some of the greatest liberals of the present time. Victorianism in my opinion is responsible for most of our troubles. It was an age of respectability, and there is nothing that is so opposed to true Christianity as respectability, pomposity, self-satisfaction, the feeling that all is well and that we are a wonderful people.

The next factor I would stress was the influence of the novelists. Novelists have been responsible for some of the most serious moral problems in this country. It is a sign of coming danger when the novelists and dramatists tend to govern thought, as they have been doing increasingly during this century. I need but mention the name of Oscar Wilde, and the harm he did. His influence was such that, by now, that for which he was condemned has become the thing to do, and you are a back number or a 'square' unless you conform to that.

Then think of the Edwardian period — that devastating Edwardian period — covering roughly the first fourteen years of this present century. The influences of Victorianism were beginning to wane, and what we now call permissiveness was beginning to manifest itself, often led by the monarch himself, who at the same time, remember, was the head of the Church of England.

These are the influences that have turned the people against religion and against God — the sham and the hypocrisy of such a type of living. Accompanying this was the increase in the number of cases of divorce. Let us not forget that divorce and the ending of marriages was first practised by, and became common among, the members of the aristocracy, not the common people. The common people have only followed and imitated their 'betters'! Those who had had the advantage of a university education, and who had been regarded as pillars of society, were the very people who in the Edwardian period began to shake the very foundations of morality and social life.

Then came the First World War. How easy it would be to demonstrate the effect that it had! Everything was shaken; nothing was the same again. Women began to work in factories and to mix more freely with men — even in the forces. Divisions and distinctions that had been always accepted were no longer recognized. There was a general lowering of standards. War always does great harm to morality. It is one of the first casualties always in war.

Then there is the whole question of the influence of the Press. The Press is, I would say, mainly responsible for the present state of morals and the troubles of society today. It has generally been just a handful of writers who have influenced the thinking of the masses — men of ability, some even of genius, who can write well. They began to poison the whole climate of thought. They did so in articles, and some of them in novels. I have noticed over the years how in particular the film and the dramatic critics have been guilty of this. I have observed that whenever a play seemed to have provided decent and innocent enjoyment the critics have always condemned it. They have ridiculed it and dismissed it as sentimental and unworthy of attention. We must have realism, they say, and so they have persistently encouraged what was once known as 'kitchen-sink' drama, and thus have gradually lowered the entire standard.

Another charge I would bring against the Press is that they have been guilty of a tendency to trivialize everything. This is a most serious matter. Side by side with something momentous, something of great importance, something very serious, they frequently put on the same front page something comparatively trivial and unimportant.

I shall never forget an example of this in 1969. I happened to be in the United States on that great day when the American astronauts landed for the first time on the surface of the moon. I noticed in the newspapers the next morning that there in bold type on the left-hand side of the front page was the account of this phenomenal achievement, but, given equal prominence on the right-hand side was an account of how some poor girl had been drowned in a lake in one of the New England states in the motor car of Senator Edward Kennedy — the Edward Kennedy whose sensitive conscience is so hurt and wounded by the presence of British troops in Northern Ireland to prevent murder and riot!

I noticed how a popular newspaper, the very day after the vote in Parliament determining our entrance into the Common Market, put that momentous news in just one column on the left-hand side of its front page, while there was a great photograph on the rest of the front page. What was it about? It had reference to a case that was on in the courts concerning another American millionaire who had given some presents to some woman, not his wife, and they were now fighting about the ownership of these jewels. When the Press behaves in that way the end result is that nothing is important.

The same thing, of course, is true of the television and the radio. There we get tragic reports of people murdered, or killed in accidents, the horrors of war, and things of that description, and then, immediately following, some nonsense, some triviality. So people shrug off death and murder and rape and vice; nothing seems to matter. Everything, as the result of the influence of the Press and these media of communication, has become so trivialized that to the masses of people today nothing is of any importance. 'On with the dance!' 'On with the motley!' Nothing matters!

But, alas, these are not the only factors that have played a part in producing this present situation. The situation is so desperate that we must face it with frankness and honesty. Can anyone absolve the church from her share in these matters? What has been the influence of ecclesiastical politics? I suggest that, far too often, it has been to make people cynical with regard to the whole of religion. They have observed that men who have taken solemn vows declaring that they adhere to certain confessions of faith and certain formulæ often preach the exact opposite and defend themselves by saying that when they took the vows they had 'mental reservations'. Is it surprising that we have the problem of dishonesty and of lying amongst young people and others, when religious leaders are guilty of the very same thing?

Even worse, we have recently had the spectacle of a bishop giving evidence in the famous trial concerning the book *Lady Chatterley's Lover* on behalf of the book, and comparing what he felt when he read it with what he experiences in the taking of the Lord's Supper. And what can we say when the leaders of the church supported in the House of Lords the putting into legal form of the Wolfenden Report recommendations with regard to homosexual practices? These are the things that have undermined the confidence of people, not only in morals in general, but particularly in the Bible, and in the teaching of the Christian faith.

Another factor, and this has been very serious also, has been the behaviour of the politicians. Nothing can so shake one's belief in honesty and integrity and in principles, as to see men changing their opinions without any apparent reason and going back on what they themselves had initiated, merely because they are no longer the government.

I am not concerned about the rights and the wrongs, or the merits, of the particular case with regard to entering into the European Common Market, but what does concern me is that when the impression is given that politicians are more concerned about party advantage and politics, and perhaps even personal advantage, than about principles, the end result is that the people in general not only lose confidence in the particular politicians, but also lose confidence in politics as such. The whole thinking of the country about government is undermined. And this, I suggest, is what has happened, the result being the present cynicism of the vast majority of people. The common attitude towards the church, and towards the state and its leaders, has become utterly cynical; and every form of Establishment is denounced and dismissed. This is what has been happening over the years; these are some of the factors and subsidiary causes which have led to the present result.

The real cause

That brings me to what I regard as the real cause, the ultimate explanation. The real trouble is *theological*. Whether you like it or not, our present troubles are ultimately theological; they cannot be understood or explained in any other manner. Here, alas, one has to say it again, the church herself has been mainly responsible. To what am I referring? It is to that which began in the thirties of the last century, and which has increased so rapidly ever since. It is what is called the 'higher critical' attitude towards the Bible. The Bible, which had hitherto been regarded in general as a revelation from God, written by men who were under the control and guidance and inspiration of the Holy Spirit, began to be regarded in an entirely new way. Revelation was dismissed and dethroned and replaced by 'reason', by the belief in man's reason and understanding called philosophy and especially, of course, science.

This is the real nerve of the problem of the contemporary situation. You cannot understand it at all unless you realize that the thinking of the vast majority of the people is governed and determined by what they regard as science. The boast is that we are living in a scientific age, the atomic age, and that we are no longer religious, and no longer believe the Bible, because of science. One of the main ways in which this attitude manifested itself was in Darwinism. Darwin's famous book, published in 1859, *The Origin of Species,* had a profound effect immediately, and that has continued and increased. People felt that the Bible had been undermined, had been proved to be wrong. Science could explain everything; God was no longer necessary.

Later in the century came the vogue of psychology, and particularly the Freudian psychology. This was atheistical and, again, an attempt to explain man in natural terms only. Another form it took was 'behaviourism', which means that everything we do is the result of some stimulus, that man is virtually but a collection of reflex-arcs, and that every action is the result of a stimulus. The followers of these schools of thought did not believe any longer in the mind. The brain yes, but not the mind. The whole of life was explained in an entirely mechanistic manner.

Others explained man in terms of the various ductless glands of the body. What made Shakespeare Shakespeare? Well, it was just that he had a little more thyroid gland than most people; Beethoven — an unusual activity of the suprarenal glands; Napoleon — excessive pituitary activity! So the idea became current that man is nothing but a kind of resultant of the operation and interaction of various forces, biological and others.

Others argue that life was purely a matter of the interplay of materialistic forces — dialectical materialism, supply and demand, and so on. Man is thus reduced to the level of a machine. It is such thinking, I contend, that has led to the present conduct and behaviour of men and women, not only in the matter of morals, but also in industry and politics and everything else.

How has it done so? This so-called 'scientific thinking' came to the conclusion that there is no such realm as the supernatural; there is nothing but this world. There is no God; there is no mind at the back of the universe: it has all just happened. It may be an original 'big bang' or 'continuous creation', but it is all in nature, all the result of natural forces: there is no mind; there is no control. The universe is an accident.

Then the great question: what is man? Oh, man is nothing but a creature, just an animal! His cerebrum may have developed a little more than that of most animals, but he is still only an animal.

This is not just a matter of my personal views. Take the following from Sir John Eccles in *Facing Reality*. He talks about scientists who claim 'that the whole of our conscious existence inevitably will be reduced to physics and chemistry'. This has been taught seriously, and it has been accepted by the majority of the people.

What of life and our way of living? There is no law, of course, no discipline; we must just obey our instincts. Man should do what the animals do. So you do not believe in law and discipline in the home, or in the school, or anywhere else; let man express himself. Self-expression! Religion, we are told, is that which has held us down, kept us back — 'the dope of the people'. At last we have been liberated, so let us express ourselves; let us show our genius, let us show what real living means without any inhibitions.

Morals — conduct and behaviour? All this is relative, we are told. There is what is described as 'situational ethics'. A well-known leader in this type of thinking, Baroness Wooton, tells us that moral standards, so called, are simply the approved behaviour patterns of the majority and that it is the business of all of us to conform to the opinions of the majority. And so it comes to this, that you must not say that something is wrong; what you mean is that it is wrong for you. It may not be wrong for me, and you must not foist your opinion on me. So-called morals are just 'the approved behaviour patterns of the majority'. You must not talk about a norm or a normal or a natural; for what is natural for you may not be natural for another man. You must not say that sex perversions are unnatural, because they are not unnatural for that particular man or woman. They are 'natural' for them.

That is the argument. Obviously therefore you have no law, you have no standard. We are all made differently; we therefore all behave differently. This becomes most serious when the lawyers accept it, and when they say that laws with respect to these matters are to be determined by the opinion of the majority. So you change the laws with regard to sex perversions, and so on. The majority opinion is the rule, is the law; this must be regarded as always right.

Still more serious perhaps, recently, is the notion of what is called 'diminished responsibility'. In other words, if you can prove, for instance, that a man was under the influence of drink when he committed a crime, you must not hold him responsible; he did not know what he was doing. Or, if you get psychiatrists and others to give an opinion in court and say that in their opinion this man was not really responsible, then he is not responsible and he must not be punished. Surely this undermines the whole concept of law? There is no norm, no standard whatsoever, and the result is that there is no self-discipline. Every man does 'that which is well-pleasing in his own sight'.

That brings us to the ultimate question—death. Inevitably, in the light of the modern outlook, the idea is that death is the end. There is nothing beyond death; there is no future life. So we need not listen to all the warnings of the Scripture. Death is the end, so when a man dies it is the same as a flower dying, a tree falling, or an animal dying.

The new attitude to man

All this has produced the modern attitude towards man and life and death, and all that ultimately matters. I am particularly concerned to emphasize that all this has been done with assured dogmatism. It has not been put forward as a theory, but claims to be based on facts. The dogmatism has been almost incredible. The view that the modern attitude towards man and life and death, and consequently to moral behaviour, is based on a totally unwarranted 'scientific' dogmatism is held not only by Christians, but also by eminent scientists who do not speak as Christians. Let me quote again from the remarkable book called *Facing Reality* by Sir John Eccles, probably the greatest authority in the world today on the brain and the way in which it works. It is a book containing a great deal of technical material, but, in addition, there are certain general statements which are of crucial importance at the present time. He writes about 'the materialistic, mechanistic, behaviouristic and cybernetic concepts of man which at present dominate research'.

Again he says, 'I have no objection to scientists expressing those views as long as they do not claim to speak with the authority of science, which is assumed by the public to provide certainties that must be accepted universally. We must instead recognize that science is in fact a personal performance of scientists.' Again: 'Science is in danger of becoming some great monster feared and worshipped by man, and carrying with it the threat to destroy man.' Still more striking: 'There is no basis at all for any dogmatic statements with respect to the nature of man while we are in our present state of abysmal ignorance.' 'The coming revolution', he goes on, 'in science will so transcend present inadequate concepts that our present science even in its most sophisticated aspects will appear as primitive and naïve.'

In another place he writes, 'Now many biologists are realizing that a kind of pseudo-religion, Darwinism, is being foisted on us, to wit that we are in a cosmic process of evolution that in principle gives a complete explanation of our origin and nature.' While he does believe in the development of the human body along evolutionary lines, he says that Darwinism does not begin to explain our self-consciousness, the thing that makes us really human.

Probably most of us will be surprised to read from this scientist: 'Arrogance is one of the worst diseases of scientists.' If I or any other Christian preacher said that, there would be an uproar, and it would be regarded as but a further example of the obscurantist ignorance of evangelical Christians. But let us continue with the quotation: 'Arrogance is one of the worst diseases of scientists, and gives rise to statements of authority and finality which are expressed usually in fields that are completely beyond the scientific competence of the dogmatist. It is important to realize that dogmatism has now become a disease of scientists rather than of theologians.'

'There is', says Sir John Eccles, 'an entrenched materialistic orthodoxy, both philosophic and scientific, that rises to defend its dogma with a self-righteousness scarcely equalled in the days of religious dogmatism.' That is the verdict of this Nobel Prize-winner scientist. That is what has been dominating the thinking of the masses of the people. It is because of this dogmatism of so-called 'science' — which is but the opinion of certain scientists, as Sir John Eccles so rightly says, and 'often outside their own particular sphere' — that people no longer believe in God, or in the real truth about man, or in the biblical teaching about living and dying.

What has been the result of all this? It has resulted, says the same writer, 'in a loss of the sense of man's true nature and man's true greatness. Mankind is sick, and has lost faith in itself and in the meaning of existence.'

He states that yet more clearly: 'There is no doubt that in general mankind has felt a downgrading of man's status in this universe during the last three or four centuries. Firstly, our earth became a mere trivial component of the universe; and secondly, man became merely a clever animal that arose by a biological process. This emotional devaluation of man is not justified by the scientific discoveries, and arises from a misunderstanding of man's real position.'

This devaluation of man, and especially of the individual, has led to the modern idea of the 'mass man'. Professor Arnold Toynbee, in his book *Surviving the Future*, has much to say about this loss of individuality, and says that 'The world is being dehumanized.' We have lost our sense of responsibility; we regard ourselves as but cogs in a wheel, a mere speck in a mass of humanity. A sense of individuality has gone, and responsibility goes with it. There is no interest in high achievements, no concern about the great qualities — love, truth, goodness, beauty, wisdom. That is what Sir Arnold Toynbee says. The vast majority do not understand these things, but have somehow gathered the impression from the men of intellect, of knowledge, and especially of 'science', that life in this world is more or less meaningless and is a matter of pleasure and of enjoyment. 'Who are we to understand?' they say. 'We are told that we are just animals; very well, let us behave as such. Let us have our enjoyment. Let us have our fling. If we are but creatures, well, life is a farmyard, so let us act as if we were in a farmyard.' That is precisely what is happening. It is the inevitable outworking of the teaching of these dogmatic 'scientists'. It has resulted in an utterly materialistic outlook; money is the great god; mammon is worshipped by almost all. Why? Because with money you can buy more food, more drink, more sex. We are living in an age of materialism, love of ease and the comforts of life, an age of gadgets.

The present turning-point

But that is not the whole story. We are, I believe, at a very interesting turning-point. Though this is the view of man, and though men have come to the conclusion that there is nothing to do but to 'eat, drink and be merry, for tomorrow we die', I sense the beginning of a reaction against all that. It manifests itself as a spirit of fear. In spite of the fact that all have washing machines and television sets and motor cars, and everything that makes life really worth living, the question arises: what if we lose it all? The very technology in which we have boasted may put us out of work. Man will not be necessary; the machine will do all. And then the horrible bombs — what if they are going to be let loose, what if there is going to be a Third World War, what if we are going to lose everything? A spirit of fear, bred of uncertainty, is beginning to appear.

This also is a vital element in our analysis of the present looseness in morals and behaviour. A sense of futility, a sense of fate, a feeling that the world may suddenly explode or collapse beneath our feet is a part of the modern outlook. This is leading to some very interesting results. One is that there is a very obvious reaction at the present time against intellectualism. Until comparatively recently intellectualism, as we have seen, and especially in the form of 'science', controlled everything. It began with the 'Enlightenment' of the eighteenth century and led on to the higher-critical view of the Bible in the thirties of the nineteenth century. The Bible was dismissed from its old position of authority and replaced by philosophy. But now there is a reaction against intellectualism, and all its sweeping claims and promises to be able to produce utopia. All it seems to have given us is two world wars and the present precarious position.

This reaction is showing itself as a wave of irrationality. This is found among the students in America, and increasingly in this country. Reason is being distrusted and set on one side. Following D. H. Lawrence many are saying that our troubles are due to the fact that we have over-developed our cerebrum. We must listen more to our 'blood' and go back to nature. And so turning against intellectualism, and deliberately espousing the creed of irrationality, they yield themselves to the desire for 'experience' and place sensation above understanding. What matters is feeling and enjoyment, not thought. Pure thought leads nowhere. Science is changing; Newton is out of date. Relativity in science has led to a doctrine of relativism in morals. Thought is a waste of time; you must enjoy yourself, seek sensation and feeling, and just obey your instincts. So they turn to sex in any form and without limit, and take alcohol and other drugs — anything that will lead to feeling, or a trip into a realm where they shall temporarily be oblivious of their troubles and problems. It is the glorification of instinct and the animal part of our nature. The moderns object even to the measure of control and discipline sanctioned by the intellectuals and the humanists. There is a reaction against all ideas of control, and a belief in sensation, instinct and even violence.

That reminds us of another form taken by this reaction, which in certain respects is much more serious. It is the advocacy of rebellion and revolution, based upon the feeling that nothing will do except we smash all we have hitherto known and introduce an entirely different manner of government — either Communism on the one hand or Fascism on the other. Both Communism and Fascism are dictatorships; both are advocated in the name of liberty, yet both would impose upon us a rigid mechanistic control which would not only not allow us to work as we choose, but also not allow us to think as we choose. In spite of what we have witnessed during this century, such ideas are still being advocated.

Some simply advocate rebellion as such, a merely negative smashing up of all we have and have known, without any idea as to what to put in its place. This is clearly the attitude of many of the students in America who are influenced by the teaching of Marcuse. The teaching is that what we have had, and what we have, must be done away with and destroyed. Then, after that, we shall face the future as best we can.

This cult of licence and lawlessness in other cases manifests itself as the filth of pornography, and even in the filth of the body. It is to be seen in the attitude to personal appearance and in the way in which people dress. The cult of the ugly is obviously attracting many devotees. The idea is, 'Evil be thou my good.' We are hearing about 'post-civilized man' and the glorification of the 'anti-hero'. Everything that is noble and elevating and beautiful is derided and dismissed. To be truly 'with it' is to protest against everything that has gone before us.

The only cure

What can be done about all this? Is there any hope? Do we just stop
at description and with diagnosis? Thank God, we do not. There is
a hope; there is a cure — but there is only one. It is the Christian
gospel message, the message of the Bible. It alone can explain why
we are as we are. It alone can expose the fallacies of all I have been
trying to describe. I maintain that this is the only hope for the reason
that everything else has already been tried. We have tried education;
we boast of our culture. We have gloried in science; we have trusted
the politicians; we have studied sociology. But look at the state of
our country! Look at the state of the world!

It is at this point, alas, that these excellent men, these great
thinkers, whom I have been quoting are as bankrupt as everyone
else. What has Professor Arnold Toynbee to offer to us, the great
historian who sees the terrible plight we are in? What is his remedy?
He tells us that we must all try to recapture the notion of love. We
have to do that, but it is the one thing we cannot do, as Rosalind
Murray showed so clearly some thirty years ago in her *The Failure
of the Good Pagan!* There is nothing more hopeless than to tell a man
that his salvation lies in his own hands. We cannot save ourselves;
we are all miserable failures.

Sir John Eccles likewise sees as our only hope that we should
understand these problems and see the fallacy of the 'scientists' who
have misled us — not science but certain scientists — and try to
come back to some kind of rationality. The problem is thrown back
to us, but the whole history of mankind demonstrates the utter
inability of man to pull himself up by his bootstraps.

The message of the Christian gospel is the only hope. But how
can this be brought to the masses? I would give a twofold answer to
that question. There is *the part that is to be played by the individual
Christian*. He can and must deal with many of the things to which
I have been referring. If he has a gift for writing, let him go in for
journalism; let him start writing. If he is a scientist, let him not be
content with merely carrying out his experiments as he is told to do
so. Let him cease to live his life in two compartments, being a good
Christian on Sunday and then leaving his Christianity at home when
he goes to his laboratory on Monday. Let him work out his beliefs
and philosophy of life in his scientific work, as Sir John Eccles and

others have been doing. Let others go into politics. These are the ways in which the individual Christian can influence the situation. Wherever he is, whatever his calling, whatever his propensities and abilities, let him apply what he believes. Let him expose the fallacies; let him try to convince his colleagues, on his own level, of the fallacy of their position and the rightness of his position. That is the way in which the individual Christian can help. I am not, I must confess, impressed by the sight of Christian people marching in protest about the streets. That has never seemed to me to be an intelligent way of dealing with any situation. Let each Christian witness in his own realm and sphere; let him bring his influence to bear there.

But when the individual Christian has done his utmost, he will not be able to achieve much. That is because, as we have seen already, the controlling idea today is that the majority determine these things. If the majority are in favour of relaxing the laws with regard to pornography, or with regard to homosexuality, well, the majority opinion is always right. So the small minority of Christian people will be able to do little. They can write, and they must; let them go on doing all they can in every way. But there is of necessity a limit to what they can do because the state only listens to the majority. While there was what was called the 'nonconformist conscience' in this country the state listened. It was a Methodist preacher called Hugh Price Hughes who really compelled Mr Gladstone to turn against Charles Stewart Parnell. How did he do so? Because of the size of the nonconformist vote in those days. There were many nonconformists at that time and the Liberal party depended upon their votes. As long as these matters are determined by counting heads, and by the majority, the state will not pay much attention to small minorities. Nevertheless, let the individual Christian do his utmost with all his might and main. Let him expose the fallacies, and especially the false dogmatism of so many 'scientists'.

What of the church herself? I draw this distinction between what the individual Christian does, and what the church does. What is *the business of the church* at a time like this? My first reply is that the church must never be, nor become, or even give the appearance of being, a protest movement. When the church is regarded as a protest movement she has become a travesty of herself. Neither must the church be a branch of the Establishment. The church is not in the world to preserve the status quo. The church was never meant to be merely the bulwark of respectability and decency. Neither is it the business of the church to improve society. All that is the business of the state; and the real tragedy of the past century has been that the church has given the impression that she is simply on the side of the Establishment and of decency and of respectability. That is not her calling.

Still less is it the business of the church to indulge in mere denunciation of sins and sinners. How easy it is to do that! The church is not to denounce the sinner, to walk on the other side of the street holding up holy hands. That is pharisaism. The church, like her Lord and Master, is to be filled with, and to show, compassion. She is to look upon these people as 'sheep without a shepherd', mauled by ravenous dogs and beasts. She is to have pity upon them, the pity that brought the Son of God from the courts of glory into this sinful world. We are to know something of this, and to show it in our lives. We are to feel a sense of sorrow, and a sense of concern. As Christians we are not simply to denounce the deluded young people and others at this present time. We are to see them as the unfortunate dupes and victims of a totally wrong attitude to life and everything noble, which has been inculcated by their teachers and mentors. We are to show great compassion and concern.

But above all, we are to bring to them a message of hope. The Christian message is a gospel, good news — not condemnation. The church's primary task is to bring men to God, and not merely to make decent citizens of them. You can be highly moral and very decent and yet be godless; but it avails you nothing in the sight of God. You remember the words of Jesus Christ. 'Ye are they', he said to the Pharisees, 'which justify yourselves before men; but God knoweth your hearts; for that which is highly esteemed among men is abomination in the sight of God' (Luke 16:15). The church has become so respectable that she has lost contact with the masses, and consequently she has become comparatively useless.

The business of the church is to preach the gospel and to produce more Christians. Then, when there are more and more Christians, their influence and their votes will count, and the state will listen. Then you will be able to repeal some of the recent regrettable Acts of Parliament. The business of the church is to preach the gospel of salvation to all and sundry. I say to 'preach' it. We need to recapture words like 'proclamation' and 'declaration'. The apostle Paul said to the learned sophisticated Athenians, 'Whom ye ignorantly worship, him I declare unto you.' The church's business is not 'to suggest', or to say that 'on the whole she thinks this', or to discuss the findings of the latest scholarship. She is to declare, 'Thus saith the Lord.' When the church confronts the world without authority, or in her own right and intellectual understanding, she is doomed to failure, and she has failed. She is to proclaim the Word and the message of God.

What is that? It starts by laying down the fundamental proposition found in the first chapter of the epistle to the Romans, in verse 18. It is that you can never have morality, true morality, without godliness. Failure to realize that has been the greatest fallacy of the past century. I remember listening to a distinguished legal luminary being interviewed on a television programme. He had been a lay preacher in his early days, so he was asked the question: 'Do you still believe that kind of thing?' 'Ah, well,' he said, 'I still hold to the ethic; but of course I no longer believe the doctrines and the dogma.' The answer to that is, that it is not only based on wrong theology, but also fails in practice. It may work for a while, as Emil Brunner pointed out years ago in *The Mediator*. The first generation is moral and holds on to the ethical teaching because it believes the truth from which the ethic is derived; the next generation holds on to it without understanding it because it no longer adheres to the truth; the third generation does not even hold on to the ethic and the morals.

Nothing can sustain morals but godliness, belief in and practice of the truth of God. The last hundred years have proved this abundantly. 'Man cannot live by bread alone.' 'Where there is no vision the people perish.' 'There is no peace, saith my God, to the wicked.' These are the words of Scripture. 'No peace'! Though you may be wealthy and learned, and cultured and sophisticated, it is still true that 'There is no peace, saith my God, to the wicked.' In spite of all our boasted advances of the last century, there is no peace in the world, there is no peace in the individual human heart. Men and women in general are unhappy; they are lost and have no sense of direction in life.

Ill fares the land, to hastening ills a prey,
Where wealth accumulates, and men decay.

The words of Goldsmith are being verified in an alarming manner at the present time.

We must proclaim this. Then we must announce the great doctrine of 'God over all'. You cannot explain the universe apart from him. Many scientists have seen and confessed that, among them the late Sir James Jeans, who said, 'There must be a great mind at the back of the universe; God must be a great mathematician.' A lifetime's study of science had driven him to that conclusion.

What about man? Sir Charles Sherrington, one of the greatest physiologists of this century, in the last year of his life in 1951 said, 'For me now the only reality is the human soul.' Another great scientist, Schrödinger the physicist, writes, 'The great question is this, Who are we?' 'The answer to this question', says Schrödinger, 'is not only one of the tasks, but *the* task of science.'

What is man? These great scientists, in contradistinction to popular science-fiction writers like the late H. G. Wells, have come to believe in the soul; nothing else matters, they say. Man is not a mere animal; he is a special creation of God. He has been made 'in the image and likeness of God'. He was not meant to live like an automaton obeying in a reflex manner every impulse and instinct within him. He has a mind and reason and understanding. He is meant to know God; and God has given man his law in order to show him the way in which he is meant to live. Man is the biggest creature in the whole cosmos, 'the lord of creation'. He is as he is today, and his world is as it is, because he does not realize this, because he has forgotten it. It is all the result of the Fall as described in the book of Genesis. It is because of man's sinful nature, because he is unregenerate. We must proclaim this.

But we must not stop even at that. We must proclaim the biblical doctrine of God's judgement upon evil and sin. If there is one note that needs to be emphasized in the modern world more than another it is the note of judgement. Why did Christ ever come into this world? He himself gave the answer: 'The son of man is come to seek and to save that which is lost.' He came because the world is under the judgement of God. The message of the Bible from beginning to end is a message of judgement. Christ did not come into the world merely to make us happy. He came to save us from the judgement to come, from 'the wrath to come'. He came to reconcile us to God. The cults are interested only in happiness, and make their lavish promises. But Christ, proclaiming that 'In the world ye shall have tribulation', has come to save us out of it and its harmful influence. That is why he gave his life 'a ransom for many'.

The most appalling aspect of the present situation is that the world does not realize that it is already under the judgement of God. I am referring to and expounding the second half of the first chapter of Paul's epistle to the Romans. There, the apostle makes a review of history and tells those Roman Christians in the first century A.D. that there had been times previously, similar to what they were experiencing, when men had worshipped one another instead of worshipping God, had 'worshipped the creature rather than the Creator, who is God blessed for ever'. What had happened? God had sent his prophets to show them their error and their sin, to plead with them to repent and to change their ways; but they would not listen. So then God 'gave them over to a reprobate mind', which means that he withdrew his restraining influences from them. He allowed man to do with man 'that which is unseemly', and woman to do with woman 'that which is unseemly'. That is the apostle's explanation of periods in world history which are so similar to the present age, when homosexuality has been elevated into something almost wonderful, better than heterosexual love. At such times God abandons men, saying to them in effect, 'If you do not listen to me and my holy law, I will let you see the consequences of your folly and your unbelief.'

I believe that we are witnessing a repetition of that in this century. I believe the two world wars were a manifestation of this, that through them God was saying to men, 'You have claimed that you would make a perfect world without me. You have done away with me. You say you can introduce perfection and paradise by means of Acts of Parliament. Very well, get on with it.' And we have had Buchenwald and Belsen, and the horrors of the two world wars. This is a part of the judgement of God.

These, however, are mere adumbrations of what is finally going to take place. As Paul said to those learned Athenians, Stoics and Epicureans, 'God now calleth all men everywhere to repent.' Why? 'For he hath appointed a day in which he will judge the whole world in righteousness by that man whom he hath ordained, whereof he hath given assurance unto all men in that he hath raised him from the dead' (Acts 17:30-32). The resurrection of Jesus Christ is in that sense a proclamation of the last judgement. The world is already under judgement, and rotting itself to perdition; but upon it all will come the promulgation of God's final sentence.

The business of the church, therefore, is to call men to repentance, and then offer the glorious gospel of salvation. She has authority to tell the world at its worst, in its rags, in the very gutters of vice and evil, that if they but repent, and believe that God sent his Son into the world, and even put our sins on him, and punished him in our stead on the cross on Calvary, and raised him from the dead in order that he might forgive us and reconcile us unto himself — that, if they believe that, they will be forgiven immediately. 'For God so loved the world that he gave his only begotten Son, that whosoever believeth in him should not perish, but have everlasting life' (John 3:16).

But, still more wonderful, we have a message that tells men that they can be 'born again', that they can have new life, and that the Spirit of God will be put in them. They will receive new power, instead of loving the darkness and hating the light.

That is literally the only hope for the world. What hope have you to offer to the drug addict? What hope have you for the alcoholic? What hope is there for men who have sinned so long that they have no will-power left? What is the point of urging them to try to recapture 'the idea of love', or to become rational, and take a new view of life and its attendant circumstances? The only hope for this sad, sick, unhappy world is to pay heed to the apostle Paul's words in 1 Corinthians chapter 6: 'Know ye not that the unrighteous shall not inherit the kingdom of God. Be not deceived: neither fornicators, nor idolaters, nor adulterers, nor effeminate, nor abusers of themselves with mankind, nor thieves, nor covetous, nor drunkards, nor revilers, nor extortioners, shall inherit the kingdom of God. And such were some of you.' But they were no longer that. Why not? 'But ye are washed, but ye are sanctified, but ye are justified in the name of the Lord Jesus, and by the Spirit of our God.' That is the only hope for your hippies, your drug addicts, your modern Pharisees — for anybody.

> His blood can make the foulest clean,
> His blood availed for me.

The Christian gospel offers new life, new power, new understanding, an entirely new orientation. Having 'the mind of Christ', the Christian sees life differently, sees death differently and looks forward to the 'blessed hope' of the glory that awaits us with God in eternity, when he shall send his Son back again into this world to 'judge the whole world in righteousness' and set up his glorious kingdom.

The business of the church is to proclaim that message, and not merely to be sending resolutions and words of advice to the prime minister or to the leader of the opposition. Let individual Christians do that, and play their full part as citizens. But not the church. She is to proclaim God's Word to parliaments and all men. We need a touch of the spirit of John Knox, in the sixteenth century, who would preach in such a manner as to cause his queen, Mary Queen of Scots, to tremble. It is said that she was more afraid of his prayers than of a battalion of English soldiers! The greatest need today is the proclamation of 'the unsearchable riches of Christ', the 'everlasting gospel'.

But it may be argued that people will no longer listen to that kind of preaching. But that has always been said. It was said before the flood, and it is true that the people of that generation did not listen. But that made no difference to the coming of the flood. The children of Israel centuries later would not listen to the warnings of the prophets, but they were carried away to the Babylonian captivity. John the Baptist and the Lord Jesus Christ himself warned their contemporaries of the doom that was imminent, and again they would not listen. But A.D. 70 came and their words were verified. The Jews were cast out of Jerusalem, their city was sacked and they remained out of it until comparatively recently.

The church is to go on preaching the Word of Christ, who said, 'As it was in the days of Noah, so shall it be also in the days of the Son of man. They did eat, they drank, they married wives, they were given in marriage, until the day that Noah entered into the ark, and the flood came and destroyed them all.' It was the same also in the days prior to the destruction of Sodom and Gomorrah, with all their perversion and foulness so like modern London. They ignored all warnings, confident that nothing was going to happen. But it did happen. And we must warn this present generation, reminding of this 'As ..., so' of the flood and Sodom and Gomorrah.

Moreover, when the church is filled with the Spirit of God they will listen. This is the glory of our position. Look at the beginning of the Christian church as described in Acts 2. Jesus Christ returned to heaven leaving his message and kingdom in the hands of just a small company of ignorant people, fishermen and others. How ridiculous it seemed! What could such men do in a world like this? But look at what they did. Our Lord, according to his promise, baptized and filled them with the Holy Spirit. As the result of that, Peter preached a sermon on the Day of Pentecost and 3,000 people were converted. They did listen; they were made to listen! But a little later these same 'ignorant' and 'unlearned men' were described in these terms: 'These men that are turning the world upside-down have come hither.' Though they were ignorant, ordinary men, being filled with the Spirit of God, they were able to turn the world upside-down.

Recently I was passing through the little town of Rhuddlan in North Wales, and I was reminded of something very relevant to our concern about the state of the nation today. It made me feel ashamed of a church that is simply petitioning authorities or protesting, and making her futile appeals to governments. Do you know what a preacher called John Elias did once in that little town of Rhuddlan towards the end of the eighteenth century? There was an annual fair held in Rhuddlan, and it was the occasion of much drunkenness and debauchery and vileness of the worst type. John Elias went there and preached a sermon, and that one sermon put an end to that fair. That is Christianity! Not mere negative protests, but putting an end to evil, 'turning the world upside-down'. How did John Elias succeed? It was not merely his natural gift of oratory; it was because he was filled with the Spirit of God and preached the message of God without fear or favour.

The supreme need of this hour is a spiritual revival, for the church to be filled with the Spirit of God. Nothing else will avail us. We need less travelling by jet planes from congress to congress, less marching in the streets, but more kneeling and praying and pleading to God to have mercy upon us, more crying to God to arise and to scatter his enemies, and to make himself known. He is still the same God — the God of Abraham, the God of Isaac and of Jacob, the God of David, the God of Isaiah, the God of John the Baptist, the God of the apostles, the God of the early Christian martyrs and confessors, the God of the Protestant fathers burnt at the stake at Smithfield, the

God of the Scottish Covenanters, the God of the Puritans, the God of the early Methodists — above all, the God and Father of our Lord and Saviour Jesus Christ! Jesus Christ is 'the same, yesterday, today, and for ever'. 'God is the Father of lights, with whom is no variableness, neither shadow of turning.'

Do we really believe in the living God? Do we believe that God can still act and change the entire situation as he has done in the past? If you do, ask him to do so, go on pleading with him until he has begun to do it; and then offer to him your praise and thanksgiving, worship and adoration. The ultimate future, we know, is safe. 'The foundation of God standeth sure.' 'Nothing can make him his purpose forego.' But plead with him in the meantime to arise and to thunder with the voice of his glory, to humble this evil generation, and especially its cynical sophisticated leaders. Then hold before them his only begotten, dearly beloved Son, whom he sent into this evil, rebellious world because of his amazing and eternal love.

8.
True and false religion

Another large congregation assembled at Westminster Chapel on 17 October 1973 to hear Dr Lloyd-Jones bring a BEC annual conference to a close. On this occasion, he concentrated on the chasm between true and false religion which he saw so clearly within the contemporary church scene.

In doing this, he was not forgetting the BEC, but setting out what he regarded as the message which it alone was standing to declare and his confessed aim was to encourage it in its struggle for the sake of the people at large who desperately needed to hear it.

We meet once more in London under the auspices of the BEC. It has been my privilege on several previous occasions to address the closing meeting of the conference which is held here every other year. This time, I think everyone will agree, we are meeting in an hour which is full of, and pregnant with, tremendous possibilities. We are meeting in a day of great confusion in our poor world, torn by wars and rumours of wars, with people bewildered and not knowing what to do or where to turn. Still more tragically, it is a time of confusion in the church. Looking back across some forty-six and a half years in the ministry, I have to confess that I have never known a time of such utter confusion in the Christian church. That is the background against which we meet together and surely our primary object and purpose should be to discover, if we can, where the British Evangelical Council fits into this scene.

You have been reminded of the formation and purpose of this council, but what seems to me to be most urgent is this: 'What is its message for this particular hour; what is its peculiar task?' It is idle to have conferences and congresses. The church has been bewildered by such gatherings for many a long year and I believe most people are thoroughly tired of them.

The times are cruel and urgent and it behoves us to know with certainty what our position and task are and what God would have us do at this particular juncture. Well now, very fortunately for us, we need not waste any of our time in setting up commissions of enquiry. That is what these big denominations are all doing and they have been doing it for many long years. They set up commissions to investigate the problem and they bring in their reports. They discuss them for years and then they have to set up another commission to investigate the first. Well, I say that as evangelical people we do not waste our time by such futilities because we know that there has 'no temptation taken you but such as is common to man'. What is happening to us today has happened many a time before. And so the essence of wisdom is to turn to the Bible to discover how men in the past, of like passions with ourselves, met similar critical situations and dealt with them. There is, of course, no lack of such material.

Tonight, I am calling your attention to one great incident in Old Testament history which seems to me, and I trust that I will be able to demonstrate to you, to provide us with a perfect parallel for the situation in which we find ourselves. Here it is in 1 Kings 18. At this time, the condition of Israel had sunk to one of its very lowest levels. This was largely due, of course, to the king at that time, whose name was Ahab. He had added to his many sins by marrying a woman of the name of Jezebel. She had led him further into sin and introduced the prophets of Baal and other false prophets into the land. As a result, the whole condition of the country was deplorable, not only religiously, but in every other sense. What we are told especially is, and this is the thing that concerns me so much, that the masses of the people were in a state of utter confusion. This is clear from Elijah's words to them in the 21st verse. We read that he 'came unto all the people and said, "How long halt ye between two opinions? If the Lord be God, follow him, but if Baal then follow him." And the people answered him not a word.' That means they did not know what to say. They were utterly confused. They were inheritors of the old religion. But here were these other teachers, these other prophets, with their religion acknowledged by the king and by the authorities. So the people were confused and utterly bewildered as

to whom they should believe and follow. That was the position. Here
you have these 850 false prophets, 400 of them belonging to Baal,
450 to Ashtoreth, the prophets of the groves, as they are described.
But standing out apart from them all and protesting was this amazing
man, Elijah. So we are here given an account of this great incident
in which he played such a prominent part.

Now the question for us is: what is the messsage of this great
incident? You are familiar with it. It is one of the well-known Old
Testament scenes, full of dramatic movement, gripping in its power.
I have, however, always felt that it is an incident that can be so easily
misunderstood. Indeed, it often has been. People generally regard
this incident in terms of Elijah and many a sermon has been preached
on his courage and on his faith. Well, that is all right, and I am not
here to detract from the greatness of this man. He has always been
one of my great heroes, and yet we must not make too much of his
courage because we find him in the next chapter running away from
a woman. He was a man of flesh as we all are. No, no! The great
message here is not primarily anything about Elijah. He plays his
part (as we must in our day), but that is not the main thing. What is
the real message here? Well, as I see it, it is the conflict between the
false and the true prophets. It is the conflict between false and true
religion. God, as it were, led this man to Mount Carmel in order that
the people, being enabled to differentiate false religion from the
true, might know exactly whom to follow and what to believe.
Elijah, I say, was used in this remarkable manner in order to do that.
Let us look first at the incident in and of itself, and then I shall try
to apply it to our present state and condition.

The characteristics of false religion

The great message, I say, is the difference between false religion and
true religion. What are the characteristics of false religion? Well,
they are all laid here before us. The first is this: *false religion always
exalts man.* 'Where do you find that?' says someone. Well, I find it
in this Baal worship and the worship of Ashtoreth. Who was Baal?
The answer is that there was no such being. Baal is the creation, or
the projection, if you like, of the thoughts and the imaginations of
human beings. There never has been such a god. He has never
existed. He is the figment of men's imagination. He has been created

by the minds of men. Now that, I say, is always the characteristic of false religion. It is man-made, man-produced, thought out by men.

Of course, that has been the great characteristic of religion in this country for the last 140 years or so. You see, it is a religion that is based on human ability, human thinking, what is called philosophy. Its basis is speculation, theorizing, human knowledge and modern science. This is what came in in the last century and has developed so rapidly in this present century. It is the popular religion of today, alas, inside so-called Christian churches as well as amongst the masses of the people. What men believe is what is being taught by certain leaders. Scholarship, learning, knowledge, in the various respects which I have indicated, have constructed a god of their own. The god in whom the vast majority of people believe is a god of their own creation. They lay it down that God cannot do this and cannot do that and then they assert that God does not do either. They have made a god in their own image. What they disapprove of cannot be true of God.

I need not keep you with this. As evangelical people you are familiar with it. People today no longer believe in the God of the Bible. Baal is the god of the twentieth century. The supernatural has been eliminated. The miraculous has gone. The Lord Jesus Christ is reduced to Jesus — a mere man. They have robbed him of his eternal sonship, his unique deity and all his miracles. They have robbed him of his atoning work, his literal physical resurrection. They have created a religion for themselves, a gospel, as they put it, for this atomic, scientific age in which we live, the age of the astronauts. It is a man-made religion and it is based entirely on men's abilities and powers and understanding. Now that is always the characteristic of false religion, as it was long ago in the days of Elijah.

What is its second characteristic? Well, the second characteristic of false religion is that *it invariably lowers and debases morality*. In the time of Elijah, Israel had fallen to such depths of vice and evil. Now that is an invariable consequence of a false religion. It follows as the night the day. You remember that in Romans 1:18 Paul refers to 'all ungodliness and unrighteousness of men'. The ungodliness always comes first, you see, and it always leads to unrighteousness.

This, of course, has been the tragedy of our age. The men who, in the middle and at the end of the last century, began to turn from the Scriptures and the old evangelical gospel, did so, they thought, in the interests of learning. As the masses were no longer illiterate and uneducated, a more learned ministry was believed to be needed, and so churches went in for scholarship, claiming that the effect of this was going to be a more moral nation. They said that the old gospel had neglected the ethical and social application and so they, with their new emphasis, were going to bring in the new Jerusalem into England's green and pleasant land. This was going to be partly done by Parliament, of course, but Parliament under the influence of nonconformist teaching and later the teaching of the Church of England. But the whole of the morals of the nation were going to be elevated. Now you and I have lived to see the result of this in terms of a mounting moral problem. I am not only thinking of divorce and things of that description, but of theft, robbery and pilfering. It becomes dangerous to walk in the streets of this city at night. There is the alcoholism, the drug addiction and all the rest. We are all familiar with it. Never perhaps has the moral problem been so acute in this country, certainly not since the days of the early part of the eighteenth century before the great Evangelical Awakening. So, as false religion did in the days of Ahab, it is doing still. False religion always lowers and debases morality.

The third and the last characteristic of false religion is what makes all this so desperately important at this present time. It is that *it always lets you down just when you need it most of all*. It was all very well as a popular religion preached by these 400 prophets of Baal and the 450 of Ashtoreth. They were probably very eloquent men and could show its superiority over the old Jewish religion. But here they are and it is a time of crisis. They are on trial on Mount Carmel; the critical moment has arrived. Their god and their religion are on trial. And do you remember what happened? It let them down, and it did so completely and entirely. 'It came to pass, when midday was past, and they prophesied until the time of the offering of the evening sacrifice, that there was neither voice, nor any to answer, nor any that regarded.' Crying to him frantically in the hour of need — dead silence! Nothing! They were left to themselves, to utter discomforture, shame and loss.

Now, my dear friends, this is what makes our being members of the BEC vitally important. The people in the world today and in our country are like those of our Lord's day whom he described as sheep without a shepherd. Attacked by marauding dogs, they are drawn hither and thither, bewildered, not knowing what to do nor where to turn, trusting in various panaceas. But a day of crisis is developing.

I am not venturing into the dangerous realm of prophecy. Too many have fallen into that pit before me. But if we are not conscious of a sense of impending doom these days, we must be impervious to the movements of the Spirit round and about us. The world is in a condition of gathering gloom. We see the breakdown of so much of what is of value and we have leading scientists telling us quite seriously and solemnly, some of whom do not even claim to be Christians, that unless something unusual happens the world is going to be face to face with a terrifying catastrophe within the next twenty years. The people who are now talking about the end of the world are not some sort of crack-brained students of prophecy — that is what they were called — they are scientists. These men are terrified, not only by the possibility of a war, a third world war, but by the pollution, the problem of ecology, and so on. They are terrified and say we may be confronted by the end of the world.

Now here is our situation. What have the people to hold on to? What will they have in the time of trial? Our Lord has already answered the question. You will find it in Luke 17. He says, 'As it was in the days of Noah, even so shall it be in the days of the Son of man.' What were they doing in the days of Noah? They were eating and drinking, marrying and giving in marriage, planting and sowing. They were having a marvellous good time and they went on doing it until the flood came and took them all away. It was the same in the time of Sodom and Gomorrah. They had nothing to fall back upon but their gods who remain silent. Darkness, gloom, despair! Christian people, have you not a heart of compassion for the ignorant masses? They are being hurtled in the direction of a final catastrophe and calamity and they are without a hope to cheer the tomb.

The characteristics of true religion

Well, those are the characteristics of false religion. But what are the characteristics of true religion? They are set here before us, with equal clarity. This is the great message of this portion of Scripture.

What is the first characteristic of true religion? It is, of course, the exact opposite of everything that I have been saying about the false. *True religion exalts God.* Elijah does not speak about himself, or his own ideas, or those of any other men. He talks about the Lord God and the religion of the fathers which he and others had inherited. He stands out, apart from all the others, and calls them back to the God whom they had forsaken. In other words, the first characteristic of this true religion is that it is not man-made at all. It comes from God. The first category is revelation. We know nothing apart from revelation. Our position is not based on what we or great thinkers have said and thought, or what science has discovered. 'Thus saith the Lord...' 'To the word, to the testimony' — to the Scriptures. We stand on this; we have got nothing else. This is the evangelical position. And if we are not in this position, we are not worthy of the name of evangelical. Revelation, and propositional truth, is the historic evangelical stand. It is the stand that is being taken by the BEC and, I would venture to say, by them alone in this country at the present time. You see, the position of the evangelical Christian is this, that he is prepared to be a fool for Christ's sake. Whatever he suffers, he says that he knows nothing apart from what God in his grace has been prepared to reveal to us. So it exalts God; it bows before him. Though it does not understand, it believes, it expounds, it proclaims. Its only authority is the Word of God. That is the first characteristic of true religion and it shines out in the whole conduct and behaviour of Elijah.

The second thing, of course, which it does is that *it elevates and stimulates morality*. 'Be ye holy, for I am holy,' says the Lord. Israel was a holy nation because they were set apart as God's people, a people for his own possession. They were to be different from all others because they were his. That is the great message, of course, which runs through the whole of the Bible from the Old Testament to the New, from beginning to end. 'Righteousness exalteth a nation.' So you have the great prophets and others teaching righteousness, calling upon the people to live a holy and a separate life. The same is also true in the New Testament. We are to live in such a way that the men and women who see us will know who we are. 'Only let your conversation be', says Paul to the Philippians, 'as becometh the gospel of Christ.' And this, of course, is something that is not only found in the Bible, and this was the effect of the gospel.

You remember, Paul gave the Corinthians a list of terrible things which kept people out of the kingdom of God. He referred to immorality, idolatry, greed and drunkenness, and so on, and then he says, 'Such were some of you, but you have been washed, you have been sanctified, you have been justified.' This is what the gospel has always done. It could take hold of men in the gutters of Corinth and other seaport towns of that ancient world, and in the gutters of Athens with all its learning, and transform them into saints, adorning the church.

This is what it has done throughout the running centuries. Look at the effect of the Protestant Reformation. It elevated the whole life of the country. Look at the time of the Commonwealth and the great influence of the Puritans. From the moral and ethical standpoint, it was one of the most noble periods in the entire history of this country, contrasted with the Restoration that followed. The same has been true of all revivals. What brought into being the great educational movement? It was the revival of the eighteenth century. What brought about the abolition of slavery? The same thing. What put an end to the horrors of children and women working in factories? The Factory Acts resulted from an evangelical conversion, that of Lord Shaftesbury. This has been the invariable rule. Once true religion is obtained and men bow down before God, morality is elevated and society is transformed from an ethical point of view.

But I come to the last and the most blessed characteristic of true religion, and it is that *it never fails*. It never fails. The false always does. This is the thing that moves one so much in reading this account. Listen to this man pleading: 'Hear me, O Lord, hear me, that this people may know that thou art the Lord God and that thou hast turned their heart back again.' He was on trial as much as the others. Then the fire of the Lord fell. Of course it did. This never fails. This is the great message of the Bible. God has pledged himself to his people: 'I will never leave thee.' 'Though my father and mother forsake me, the Lord will take me up.' And this has been the testimony of God's people throughout the ages and the centuries. 'In every high and stormy gale, my anchor holds within the veil.' 'Nothing shall be able to separate us from the love of God which is in Christ Jesus our Lord.' It does not matter what it is: 'Neither death, nor life, nor angels, nor principalities, nor powers, nor things present, nor things to come, nor height nor depth nor any other creature.' God will never forsake his people. When we need him most of all he will be there.

Now, this, it seems to me, is all-important at this present time. Look at the masses of the people. They are beginning to acknowledge the worthlessness of their false relgion. What has their false

religion to give them in the hour of their greatest need? What does
it give them when they are taken ill, desperately ill? What has it to
give them just before some serious operation? What has it to say to
them when they know that they are dying? What has it say to them
when they are bereaved and lose someone who is dearer to them than
life itself? And they are beginning to acknowledge and confess that
they have got nothing. In the hour of the greatest need — silence!
But with true religion, God is with us, in life and in death. 'All the
way my Saviour leads me,' and he will never leave us nor forsake
us.

The message for today

Very well, then, there is the general message, as I see it, of this great
chapter in the first book of Kings. But what is its message in
particular for us at this moment? We must apply this to ourselves.
That is why principles are laid down for us in Scripture. So what is
its peculiar message for us? Well, I say again, that we find ourselves
in a condition which is amazingly like the one depicted in this great
chapter. I say once more that I have never known such confusion in
the world and in the church. And, if I may say so, the confusion that
alarms and troubles me most of all is the confusion amongst
evangelical people. I believe the masses of people in our churches
are utterly confused. Why? Because of the discordant voices, the
contradictory voices that come to them. They do not know where
they are or what to believe. They tend to think in terms of personalities. I remember very well, and I have said this often, what people,
evangelical people, used to say about the late Pope John. Having
seen him on television, he seemed to them to be a nice old man and
consequently, I think they were prepared to swallow everything he
had got to say. That is emotional thinking. Our people are confused
because they think emotionally about religious leaders. They say, 'I
cannot believe that so-and-so could possibly say anything wrong.'
And that settles the matter for them.

So, I say, there is this tragic confusion. Well, what are we to do?
I believe the call to the BEC, which it has heard and already
responded to, is to do in our own age and generation precisely what
Elijah did on Mount Carmel. That is why I am glad and proud to
belong to it. What is this great call? It is to help the people who are

in this state of terrible confusion to understand the issues and to know what exactly they are to do. And I believe the greatest need for this exists among those evangelicals who are still left in the big, mixed denominations. They are of all people the most mixed and confused. They are evangelical, of course they are. But they are hearing other voices and their leaders tell them to stay among such people. They are bewildered and uncertain. That is the position.

But, you know, the analogy between the text and our situation is very close — even down to the smallest details. You remember, I mentioned that Elijah stood alone, with 850 on the other side. The BEC is a very small body, you know. The big battalions are on the other side and we seem to be a despised little remnant. Thank God for the comfort and the consolation of the Scriptures. 850 false prophets and one man of God standing on his own! Yes, but let me show you another interesting thing in the analogy. I read, 'It came to pass when Ahab saw Elijah that Ahab said unto him, "Art thou he that troubleth Israel?"' Note that Ahab regarded Elijah as the cause of trouble. But do you remember Elijah's answer? It was: 'I have not troubled Israel, but thou and thy father's house, in that ye have forsaken the commandments of the Lord and thou hast followed Baalim.' But, you see, the charge was that he was the troubler of Israel. 'Look here,' they said, 'why should you stand out? Why should you be different? Why do you not join us? This is where the crowd is; we are the majority. Why should you be on your own?' They regarded him as an awkward man, who thought that he alone was right. You are familiar with the jokes that are hurled at such people.

Well, you know, that is exactly what is being said today. Why this BEC? Why not join the other evangelicals? Because they are mixed up with infidels and sceptics and denials of the truth. They are! Every other evangelical organization that I am aware of consists of those who are mixed up in their denominations with people who deny the truth as much as the prophets of Baal did. They deny the deity of Christ! And some of them are principals of theological colleges. Now this is the tragedy. But, you see, if you protest, if you stand out and say, 'I cannot belong to this,' you are regarded as a troubler in Israel, someone who is causing disagreement amongst friends. If you today make a plea for evangelical unity you will be charged with dividing evangelicals. The man who stands for the truth is the troubler of Israel. But there is nothing new about this.

And so I say again, thank God for the comfort and the consolation of the Scriptures.

But what are we to do? Now then, here is the message for us: we are to start by challenging and by fighting. *It was Elijah who took the initiative.* It was he who met Ahab and who called upon him to produce his men and to go up and face the challenge. And I believe that we have reached this stage. We are not to be merely on the defensive as evangelicals, nor are we to be merely negative. And I thank God that there are things happening today which give me great encouragement. There has been a great fight in a section of the Lutheran church in the USA. It is known as the Missouri Synod — the most evangelical part of the Lutheran church in America. Their college had got into wrong hands, into liberal hands. They departed from the faith of the man who founded that synod in the last century, a man of the name of Walton. There has been a great struggle. But the evangelicals took courage and they fought out the issue in their synod and they won a victory. And I have very little doubt that before long the Missouri Synod will be divided into true evangelicals and those who are not, and the others can go and join the other branches of the Lutheran church that have already succumbed to the modernistic and liberal influence.

And another thing (I am telling you this for your encouragement, my friends): this year over 200 evangelical churches in the Southern Presbyterian churches of the USA have seceded from the denomination and have formed a new Evangelical Presbyterian Church. Over 200 — and more are coming out every week. Now these, I say, are things that gladden one's heart. Here are our brethren, across the Atlantic, fighting, standing for the faith, not cowering in a spirit of fear, but standing up for the truth and challenging its foes.

I believe that we have got to do exactly the same thing. Elijah challenged these people. And the time has come for us to challenge all those who are not truly evangelical. But notice another thing that he did: *he ridiculed them.* Do you regard ridicule as unchristian? Well, if you do, you have not read your Bible properly. I like the ridicule and the sarcasm. Do you remember what happened? 'It came to pass at noon, that Elijah mocked them, and said, Cry aloud: for he is a god; either he is talking, or he is pursuing, or he is on a journey, or peradventure he sleeepeth.' 'Wake him up,' says Elijah, 'he must be asleep! All 850 of you have said that he is a god, and you are eloquent men and the people have believed you.' So he mocked them and he ridiculed them. I believe we have got to do the same. We can do it in a spirit of love, but we must do it. What of the much-vaunted assured results of higher criticism and the methods which have been followed for some 140 years? Look at the books that have come out; look at the articles that have been written; look at the sermons that have been preached. What has it all achieved? What has all this great supposed scholarship really given us in a practical sense? Is it not time that we challenged all these claims of the false prophets and their false teaching? If there is anything that is more evident than anything else in the modern world, it is the failure of liberalism and modernism in the church. It has emptied the churches and reduced the country to its present moral level. What has been the result of the much-vaunted social gospel? Never have the social conditions been more deplorable. It is crying out. We must get up and we must open the eyes of the people. As Elijah did, we must mock these false prophets and expose them for what they are.

So we must come to the positive. What is that? It is found in the 30th verse: 'And Elijah said unto all the people, Come near unto me. And all the people came near unto him. And he repaired the altar of the Lord that was broken down. And Elijah took twelve stones, according to the number of the tribes of the sons of Jacob unto whom the word of the Lord came, saying, Israel shall be thy name: and with the stones he built an altar in the name of the Lord.'

We must do this again. What does it mean? Well, being interpreted, it means that *we have got to tell people that there is only one way to worship God*. It is via the altar that God himself has commanded. He commanded the children of Israel how to do this. They had neglected it and the altar had fallen down and was in disrepair. They repaired it and erected it again in God's way. God had told them how to build an altar in order that they might know how to worship him, how to offer their sacrifices and how to come into his presence. It is our constant task to make this known. Men and women are in desperate trouble, and in their need they tend to try God out and turn to him. We read during the last war so often, did we not, of poor men whose ships had been torpedoed? They had been in dinghies on the Atlantic for many, many days and had tried everything and did not know what to do next. Death was coming nearer and nearer and someone said, 'Can we try prayer?' But how can a man pray? How can a sinner approach God? How can one dwell with that burning light? Who can appear before the Lord?

Who shall ascend into his holy hill? We alone know the answer to that question and we are custodians and guardians of this truth. There is an altar and a sacrifice. There is a way to God: 'Having therefore, brethren, boldness to enter into the holiest by the blood of Jesus, the new and the living way.' That is what is meant by repairing the altar. We must declare again, in its fulness, God's way of salvation. There is no other: 'There is none other name under heaven given among men, whereby we must be saved.' We must be dogmatic. In an age that talks about a world congress of religions, we must say that there is only one way to God: 'I am the way, the truth, and the life: no man cometh unto the Father but by me.' It is an exclusive, intolerant gospel. 'Though we, or an angel from heaven, preach any other gospel unto you than that which we have preached unto you, let him be accursed,' says Paul. And we must say the same. An exclusive gospel — the only altar that is recognized by God.

But Elijah did not stop at that. The next thing is the most important of all. He told them three times, you remember, to pour water on the sacrifice, and so on. Then I read: 'It came to pass at the time of the offering of the evening sacrifice, that Elijah the prophet came near, and said, Lord God of Abraham, Isaac, and of Israel, let it be known this day that thou art God in Israel, and that I am thy servant, and that I have done all these things at thy word. Hear me, O Lord, hear me, that this people,' this poor benighted blinded people, 'may know that thou art the Lord God and that thou hast turned their heart back again.' Prayer, my friends, and *prayer is the most vital thing of all.* Without this the rest is useless. But am I being unduly critical when I suggest that there is very little prayer today? This is the last thing that is mentioned. Everything else comes first. But this is the most vital thing of all. As I look at the church today, what I see her doing is arranging conferences, congresses and evangelistic efforts. I am sorry to have to say it, but I am reminded more of the behaviour of the prophets of Baal than I am of Elijah. Listen, 'They cried aloud, and cut themselves after their manner with knives and lancets, till the blood gushed out.' And not only that, but they had been jumping on the altar. Tremendous activity and shouting! I am reminded too forcibly of all that as I see all this travelling in jets and this squandering of money on these big organizations, but very little mention, if any, about prayer. And yet prayer is the greatest essential of all. What place does prayer have in your life, my friend? What place does it have in the life of your church?

But wait a minute, we must know how to pray. Look at Elijah. Notice his confidence, his assurance. There is nothing frantic or desperate about him. He just said to all the people, 'Come near to me.' And they came and he began to pray with this amazing confidence and assurance, and not with the screeching and shouting of the false prophets. The quiet confidence of this man of God is remarkable. There is an incident here that I like very much. You remember that he told them to make a trench around the altar and then he told them to pour water into that trench. 'Fill four barrels', he said, 'with water and pour it on the burnt sacrifice, and on the wood. And he said, Do it the second time. And they did it the second time. And he said, Do it the third time. And they did it the third time. And the water ran round about the altar; and he filled the trench also with water.' What confidence! This God can lick up water as he can burn any shavings of paper that you may put in his track. What is his confidence based on? Is it self-assurance? Certainly not. It is his confidence in God. He knows that God is the living God, the all-powerful God.

I like his appeal to history. If you feel shaky and you are lacking in confidence when you pray, read history, my friends. The best preparation for prayer, I often feel, is the reading of history. 'Lord God of Abraham, Isaac, and of Israel!' The God who had called these men, the God who had acted in their lives, the God who had spoken to them, the God who had told them what to do, the God who had directed them, is the God of Israel. History substantiates this. But let us remember this: he is the Lord God of Abraham, Isaac and of Israel. The point that Elijah makes is this: *he is still the living God.* He is not a museum God. He is the living God. As he acted in the days of Abraham, Isaac and Israel, he can still act. That is the point that Elijah makes. He still intervenes and acts.

Christian people, I regret to ask this question, but I am constrained to do so. Do you believe in a God who still acts, or are you a proponent of the view that God stopped acting at the end of the apostolic age, and that now that we have the Scriptures, we just apply them? Is that your position? Or do you say that every man when he is regenerate receives all that he will ever receive directly from God? You do not expect any descent of the Spirit upon you. You have had all that and so you just surrender to what you have. If

that is your creed, I am not surprised that the church is as it is. Has
God stopped acting? Has God ceased to intervene? 'No, no!' says
Elijah. 'You who acted in the time of Abraham, Isaac and of Israel,
you can still act. You are still the same, and I ask you to do it now
as you did it then.' You and I must come to this, and we are fortified
in saying so by the long history of revivals in the past. Had the church
had everything on the Day of Pentecost? Pentecost as an outpouring
of the Spirit has been repeated many times. That is what we mean
by revival. The Reformation was a revival. God poured forth his
Spirit and the Spirit came down upon the people. God acted and
intervened. He also did so in the Evangelical Revival and in many
another revival since those great days. Christian people, do you
expect God to do anything? Or is it really just left to us and the Word
we have?

Listen to the plea of this man, and let me emphasize that he is
pleading for one thing: 'Hear me, O Lord, hear me.' Oh, the
importunity of this man! It is not a casual prayer, not a perfunctory
prayer, not just going to the prayer meeting as a matter of a duty, but
laying hold on God, pleading with him. 'Oh', he says, 'hear me, O
Lord, hear me.' I hear very little of this pleading and importunity
these days. Our prayers are often sermons. We have lost the art of
pleading with God, drawing on his promises, reminding him of his
greatness and his glory and pleading with him. This is what we must
restore.

But what is the plea? The plea is, 'Let it be known … that thou
art God in Israel, and that I am thy servant, and that I have done all
these things at thy word.' What was his plea? That God should
authenticate himself; that God should manifest his glory and his
power; that God should send the fire. And that is our greatest need
today: this fire from God. Nothing else authenticates. The God that
answers by fire, let him be the God. This is the test. The others are
good on paper. And if our God is only a God on paper we have
nothing to say to the people, and that is what they hurl in our teeth,
is it not? They say, 'You orthodox people, your churches are no
better than ours. I visit them and they are dead, they are lifeless.'
Shame on us if it is true! We need the fire, my friends. 'He shall
baptize with the Holy Ghost and with fire.' We need the life, the
energy, the power, the vigour, the manifestation of God. Nothing
else will authenticate our message. Oh, that is Paul again, is it not?
He said in 1 Corinthians 2:4-6, 'I came among you not with enticing

words of man's wisdom, but in demonstration of the Spirit and of power.' And I tell you good people tonight what I have said many times from this pulpit and will say again: you can organize your campaigns; you can join and amalgamate your churches; you can bring out books; you can work as frantically as these false prophets — and nothing will happen, until the church and the world are confronted by a phenomenon. And a revival is a phenomenon only to be explained in terms of the fire of God descending and a moribund church recharged with life, set upon her feet and able to speak without fear to the people. Nothing else! We have tried everything else. Look at this century, with its frantic activities. And the church goes down from bad to worse. Chapels and churches have been and are being shut; and it will continue until we come to our senses, stop many of our activities and pull ourselves together and turn to the living God and plead with him to authenticate himself and to send down the fire upon us.

What happens then? Well, here it is, you see. The fire of the Lord fell. But tell me, my dear friends, do you know anything about the falling of this fire when you are praying? It is the most blessed experience a human being can ever have. When you are praying, the fire falls and you know that he is there. You are in the presence of the living God. So the fire fell and consumed the burnt sacrifice and the wood and the stones and the dust, and licked up the water that was in the trench. And note that when the poor confused people who did not know whether they were to follow Baal or God saw the fire — what happened to them? Did they sit back in their thousands and enjoy the pop singing and the entertainment? No.

They fell on their faces. *They fell on their faces.* We need to be humbled, my friends. We, evangelical people, need to be humbled to the floor, to the dust. They fell on their faces. Have you ever been on your face? How many of our churches have been on their faces? They fell on their faces and they said, 'The Lord, he is the God; the Lord, he is the God.' Of course he is!

Let us note the final word. How vital it is! Elijah said unto them, 'Take the prophets of Baal, let not one of them escape. And they took them and Elijah brought them down to the brook Kishon and slew them there.' *We must destroy the false prophets and their teaching.* If your revival is not to be ephemeral and end in nothing, you must follow this right through and destroy the false. You must get rid of the heretics. The tragedy of the present hour is that the church has tolerated the heretics. 'We are going to win them,' they say. 'We are in it to win it. Give us time and we will win them.' Are they winning them, or being lost to them? You cannot save these heretics, these prophets of Baal. You must destroy them and their teaching. And if you cannot excommunicate them because of your numerical weakness, you have got to move yourself from their midst. That is what has happened through the centuries. It happened at the Reformation. Luther, Calvin and the rest came to realize that the church of Rome could not be reformed, and they left. The early nonconformist fathers in this country did the same thing. The Methodists eventually had to come out. The conservatism of John Wesley had held them in for years. Almost the moment he died they went out. It is essential. You cannot put new wine into old bottles. The only occasion that you will find in the history of revivals when a revival has not led to a separation has been when the church has held to orthodox doctrine and the fire has come upon that. There is no need to separate then. But when the church has gone wrong, secession follows. The secession from the Church of Scotland in 1843 is said to be one of the direct results of the revival under William Charles Burns and Robert Murray M'Cheyne. Of course, it is inevitable. The false teaching cannot be mixed with the true. The Spirit will not come down when the prophets of Baal are in control and mainly in evidence. We have to destroy the prophets of Baal.

I end on a word of warning. As I see things today, there are two dangers for us. The first is the danger of just restoring the altar, bringing back the orthodox truth, fighting the erroneous and the spurious, and stopping at that. That is essential. Elijah did it. And we must do it. We must contend for the faith. We must restore the faith to the churches and to the people.

But if you stop at that you will have a dead orthodoxy. And it will not be a phenomenon and it may lead to stagnation, to a kind of living death. That is one danger. But there is another one. There are people who are saying that nothing matters but the fire. They are not concerned about destroying the prophets of Baal. 'No, no!' they say. 'What does it matter what a man believes as long as he has this experience?' Experience only. And they say that if you have this experience, you can go on having fellowship with the Virgin Mary, a deeper experience of the mass and appreciation of the Holy Father than ever before. This is what is being taught: fire only; experience only. No restoring of the altar and the absolute truth of the Word, with the necessity of the Spirit illuminating it. No proclamation of it without fear or favour. No, no! The true position is to have both — the altar and the fire.

And if you have one without the other it will avail you nothing. We must erect the altar, and then we must pray through it, pleading with him for the fire. And if we do so in honesty and sincerity we have his promise behind us. The fire will fall. God will again have vindicated himself and his eternal truth and we shall be filled with a spirit of rejoicing. We shall see masses of people coming out of a sad, disillusioned world that is turning to drugs, to Buddhism and mysticism, clutching at any kind of experience in its utter bankruptcy. They will come to see, as these people did on Mount Carmel, that the Lord is God. The Lord, he alone is God. So, Christian people,

From strength to strength go on,
Wrestle and fight and pray.
Tread all the powers of darkness down
And win the well-fought day.

Still let the Spirit cry
In all his soldiers, 'Come,'
Till Christ the Lord descend from high
And take the conquerors home.

9.
The sword and the song

9 November 1977 saw the Doctor once more in his former pulpit, speaking for the BEC ten years after his famous (or notorious) Luther address. It was an occasion when he reviewed the decade which had passed and he had some staggering disclosures to make concerning the wider evangelical scene.

In the course of what he had to say, he described the Evangelical Alliance as being largely dominated by Anglican evangelicals. Today, that is no longer the case, numerically. However, the larger point that he made is still valid in that the breadth of views he referred to are still found within the membership of the Alliance.

I need scarcely say that I regard it as a privilege and a great honour to be asked once more to deliver an address under the auspices of the BEC. You have already heard of some little part that I was privileged to play in making this excellent council better known amongst the evangelical churches in this country and I hope to make some further reference to that fact in a moment or two. I want to base what I have to say on verses 5 and 6 in Psalm 149. They read: 'Let the saints be joyful in glory: let them sing aloud upon their beds. Let the high praises of God be in their mouth, and a two-edged sword in their hand.' I want particularly to deal with the double exhortation in that sixth verse: 'Let the high praises of God be in their mouth, and a two-edged sword in their hand.'

It sems to be the fashion at the present time to make a review of the events of the past ten years, and as we believe in being in the fashion, it is not a bad thing for us to do the same thing. It was in 1966 that I spoke at a meeting in the Central Hall here in Westminster under the auspices of the Evangelical Alliance. I ventured to make an appeal then to evangelical people, in view of certain tendencies that I had observed, to come together out of the mixed denominations and churches in which they were found so that we might make a great stand together for the truth of the gospel. My appeal was not given what one might call a friendly reception, as some of you doubtless may remember. But I did not expect anything different.

The history of that meeting and this one really goes back even further than 1952, when the BEC came into being. It goes back to the formation of the World Council of Churches in 1948 and to the attitude towards it which the Evangelical Alliance subsequently adopted. The Evangelical Alliance had functioned as a kind of co-ordinating body, keeping evangelical people together on a common basis, but it decided to adopt a position to the World Council of Churches which it described as 'benevolent neutrality'. To me that was the real turning-point. I felt that I could no longer belong to that body nor function in connection with it. It was, of course, an anomalous position for the Evangelical Alliance to take because it has, almost from the beginning, been governed by Anglican evangelicals and the Church of England was already a constituent member of the World Council of Churches. Anglican evangelicals were therefore in the ridiculous position of being in the World Council and also in a position of benevolent neutrality with respect to it. Well, it was from there on that things became clearer and so, as we have been told, we felt that we must all come together. To me, the most important point was the meeting that was held in this church in the autumn of 1967, when we commemorated together the 450th anniversary of Luther's nailing his Ninety-five Theses to the door of that famous church — what was really the beginning of the Protestant Reformation. From that meeting, this British Evangelical Council has gone on from strength to strength.

I want to review with you what has happened since then. As I say, others have been doing this and I feel that we must do it. Can we justify what we did at that time? Can we really justify the existence of this British Evangelical Council? I think it is necessary that we should deal with this because there are still some people who regard us as being divisive. They feel that all who claim to be evangelical in any sense should be together and meet from time to time to make common cause, as was done previously under the auspices of the

Evangelical Alliance. So we have got to justify what we did then, have continued to do and what we propose to go on doing. I think it is also important that we should convince certain doubters amongst ourselves. Travelling around as I do now, I still find certain people in evangelical churches who are not altogether happy at the fact that we no longer meet together as we used to do with certain evangelical brethren who have remained either in the Anglican Church or some of the other mixed denominations. It is important that they should be convinced.

There is a further reason for making this review. It is that we may be in a position to answer certain overtures that are going to be made to us to reconsider the whole question and to join once more organizationally in common activities with those who still remain in the mixed denominations. Incidentally, may I say in passing, I hope that none of you are guilty of referring to those denominations as the main-line denominations. That is what they are so often called. It is a misnomer. They are not on the main line. They have gone astray. They are not main-line denominations; they are mixed denominations. Let us therefore give them the right designation.

Well, now then, how can we justify the work and the continuation of the BEC? I propose to do so in terms of this text that I have taken. I am going to review the last ten years and show you that what we did a decade ago was not only right then, but that it has been more than justified by subsequent history. Indeed, it is never more necessary than it is at this present moment. What is the call, then, that comes to us as evangelicals in the BEC? I believe it is put before us in the double exhortation of Psalm 149:6. I am going to reverse the order of the text.

The sword

Let us consider first that we must have a two-edged sword in our hands. That means that we have to fight. Now, I am free to confess that I would have much preferred to preach to you as saints and to encourage and gladden you by reminding you of the glories of the gospel. But the business of the preacher is not to do what he feels like doing, nor even what he would really like to do. It is to deal with the circumstances as they exist and to give a message which really meets the situation in which we find ourselves. So, I am compelled to start with the sword and to remind you that we are in a fight. This is unfortunate, but it is true. We are actually commanded to do this in Scripture, in the New Testament as well as the Old, and I want to emphasize that we are all to be involved in it. It is not something that is merely for preachers or ministers. It is the responsibility of every church member. That is why I asked my friend, Dr Kendall, the minister of this church, to read that portion of Scripture where the apostle is reminding those churches at Colosse and elsewhere that they were involved in a struggle. Similarly, when writing to the Philippians, he reminded them that they were set with him both in the defence and the confirmation of the gospel. Nothing is more unfortunate than that church members should think that they are not involved in a battle of this kind. You are all in it. We are in it together and it is important that we should all know exactly what we have to do.

Now, as we have to take a sword and fight, the first question we must ask is, *'Whom are we to fight?'* This is very important. Whom are we to fight? I want to make clear that we who belong to the BEC are not meant to fight one another. I have been reminded a few times comparatively recently of something I remember the late Sir Winston Churchill saying, with respect to Mr Aneurin Bevan, the man who was responsible for housing in the Labour Government after 1945. I remember Mr Churchill, as he then was, saying that Mr Bevan was so busy throwing bricks at the builders with whom he was supposed to be co-operating that he had no time to build houses. And there was a great truth in that. Here was a man who was responsible for building houses but, instead of working with the builders, he was always attacking them. God forbid that that should be true of us! We have a common enemy and we must not dissipate our energies in fighting one another.

So that brings me to the second point. *What are we to be fighting about?* What is the cause of the battle? Here we come to the tragic part of this story. Of course, as evangelicals, we have got to fight the old liberalism and modernism, the old unbelief with which we have always had to contend and which is as obvious today as it has ever been. Think of a book like *The Myth of God Incarnate* and the things that have been given such publicity on the radio and television. That is quite obvious, as is the state of the country and its low morals.

Until about ten years ago, we were engaged in this fight with other evangelicals in the mixed denominations, that is, those represented by the Evangelical Alliance. But now — and this is the important matter of which I have to remind you — the situation unfortunately has taken a very sad and a very tragic turn. Because we must know exactly what we have got to fight, exactly what we are confronted by, I must say something I deeply regret having to say. Whatever you may think of me, I am not a natural fighter. I am a man of peace. My greatest defect is that I am too patient with people. So I would much prefer not to be saying this kind of thing, but we are here to face facts because the times are evil. The circumstances are desperate.

What is this new factor? Well, it is what has happened during these past ten years, and it is one of the most surprising stories I have ever known. When I spoke in 1966, I was aware of certain trends and tendencies. But, in my wildest moments, I never imagined that the things which have taken place in the last ten years would come to pass. It is almost incredible. But, before I deal with them, there are two good things I want to mention and register for which we should thank God. They have helped the BEC. The first is the departure of a group of evangelical Congregational churches from, first of all, the Congregational Church of England and then the so-called United Reformed Church. We have now a body of Congregational churches that are constituent members of this BEC, and I think it is only right that we should thank God for these men. They are not great in number but they are great in courage and in their stead-fastness and loyalty to the truth.

I want to give you a justification for what they did because they have been much criticized. This is what I read in an article written by one of the leaders of old Congregationalism who is now one of the present leaders of the URC. This is what he wrote: 'This union', he says, 'was hailed with generous goodwill by the other churches.' Listen — this is a Congregationalist speaking, a successor of the men ejected in 1662. He says, 'No one who was present at the inauguration of the United Reformed Church in Westminster Abbey is likely to forget the moment when the Archbishop of Canterbury, the Cardinal Archbishop of Westminster and the moderator of the Free Church Federal Council pledged themselves to pursue together that fuller unity of which the United Reformed Church was a small foretaste.' That by a Congregationalist! All honour to the men who said, 'We have nothing to do with this.' Do you realize what it means? The successors of the Puritans and of the Dissenters, the successors of those 2,000 brave men who were ejected in 1662, having an inaugural meeting in Westminster Abbey and boasting of the presence of the Archbishop of Canterbury and the Roman Catholic Cardinal Archbishop of Westminster! I remember how at the time, as part of the service, they had what they called a fanfare of trumpets, which was meant to be an emblem of rejoicing. I ventured to describe it at the time as the *Last Post,* for that is precisely what it was. It was the death-knell of what they, at any rate, regarded as Congregationalism. Well, I say, all honour to these men.

Something similar is to be seen in the case of the men who, in the last ten years, left the Baptist Union to form an evangelical association of Baptist Churches. Why did they leave? Well, I can tell you why they left. They left because a principal of one of their theological colleges, recognized by the Baptist Union, had blatantly and openly denied the deity of Christ and many of the other foundational articles of the Christian faith. But, you may say, surely the Baptist Union did something about this man? Well, what it did, at the instigation of some of the evangelical members of the executive, I understand, was to pass two resolutions. The first was to say that the Baptist Union executive still adhered to the old, evangelical doctrines and the creeds of the Christian church. Here they were proclaiming that they were still evangelicals. But then there was a second resolution. What was that? It was that the executive also asserted that it still believed in complete freedom of opinion, liberty of conscience for every man to be allowed to believe what he wants and to act according with his conscience. In other words, in Resolution 1 you say that you condemn Principal Taylor for his heresy, but in Resolution 2 you say that you still believe that he has a right to teach it. Now, at that point these men and their churches left the union and formed an evangelical association of Baptist Churches which is affiliated to the BEC. All honour to them. Would that we had further items to add to our list of good things that have happened during the last ten years but, alas, there is nothing more to say.

Let me come to the other side, the sad side, and here I shall be referring almost entirely to what has been happening amongst Anglican evangelicals. Let us make no mistake about this: the Evangelical Alliance is, in essence, an evangelical Anglican body. There are a few non-Anglicans in it but predominantly it is Anglican in membership and outlook. Of necessity therefore, I shall have to deal mainly with what has been happening in those circles, for it represents also the position of the Evangelical Alliance.

What has taken place? Well, certain books have been published. The first is a book bearing the title *Growing into Union*. It was written by two Anglo-Catholics and two evangelicals. They expressed wonder at the agreement they discovered; their fondness for one another now that they had met; their bitter regret that they had been opposed for so long and their intention not to be separated again. Two Anglo-Catholics and two evangelicals! I must not go into the contents of the book, but that was the first shattering event that took place during this period. Since then, another book has been published called *Christian Believing*. This is a report of a commission to deal with the doctrine of the Church of England, the nature of the Christian faith and its expression in Holy Scripture and the creeds. I shall refer to it further. Then a famous congress was held in the city of Nottingham — Nottingham 1977 is what it is called. I shall have to refer to this also. In addition, the so-called charismatic movement has been making certain statements with regard to the place of the importance of doctrine. Furthermore, a book has been published called *A Dictionary of New Testament Theology*, in which evangelical scholars have co-operated with well-known modernistic and liberal scholars, mainly from Germany. Evangelicals have co-operated with them in producing this book and there have also been numerous books and articles in magazines, all pointing in the same direction.

What is the meaning of all this? Well, it means that there has been a real change and a definite shift in the whole position of Anglican evangelicalism. It is, I say, almost incredible. Where has the shift taken place? First, it has taken place in *their view of Scripture*. At the Keele Conference in 1967, their concern in dealing with Scripture was with regard to its meaning. In Nottingham, ten years later in 1977, their emphasis is now upon the interpretation of the Scripture, what they call hermeneutics. I shall have more to say about that in a moment.

What has really happened is that a great change has occurred in the attitude of evangelicals, not only with regard to Scripture, but also regarding *tradition*. 'Scripture and tradition' is the old position of the Roman Catholic Church, in which Scripture is not accorded absolute supremacy. *Sola Scriptura* is denied. They have also adopted higher-critical methods in the study of the Scriptures. Read the foreword to this report, entitled *Christian Believing*. It was written by the present Archbishop of Canterbury, a man who wrote the first account of the IVF. We had lunch together on VE day on May 8 1945, meeting as evangelical friends to discuss certain questions. But this is what he writes now. He says, 'I take this opportunity of recording my thanks to the chairman and the members of the Doctrine Commission of the Church of England for the care in which they have examined the nature of the Christian faith and its expression in Holy Scripture and the creeds. The unanimity of the report was not easily achieved.' Why not, we may ask? Because on this commission there were two evangelicals, both well-known, there were Anglo-Catholics and there were extreme liberals, the most extreme imaginable. Actually, the chairman of the commission was a man who has indeed become notorious for his attitude towards the essentials of the Christian faith. His name is Professor Maurice Wiles, the Regius Professor of Divinity in the University of Oxford. Well might the archbishop be grateful for the unanimity of the report. He also says, 'The individual essays which comprise the latter part of the book show the variety of gifts and outlooks of the various contributors. That is indeed a source of enrichment for us who can now read the finished work. Each generation needs men who in honesty and devotion are prepared to undertake exploration into God, to press beyond the confines of what we hitherto have grasped and to move away from places that have become too narrow for us in the light of modern knowledge and experience. The members of the commission have sought to do just this. And I for one am grateful.' That was the kind of thing that we, as evangelicals, including this very man, used to oppose when it was written by the Student Christian Movement which was the non-evangelical, liberal, modernist movement amongst students. That is what I mean by a shift having taken place.

But, for me to deal with this point as briefly as I can, there are two other books which have recently been published. One is called *The Battle for the Bible*. Its author is the editor of the well-known magazine *Christianity Today*. The other is called *Fundamentalism* by Professor James Barr, now also of Oxford. All I have got to say is this: if you read those two books you will find irrefutable evidence that evangelicals have moved to a liberal position in their attitude towards, and their interpretation of, the Scriptures. They have crossed the line and they are adopting the methods of the higher criticism which we all opposed together so strenuously over the years.

The second evidence of this shift is that there has been a change even in the question of *the truth of salvation and the truth concerning the church*. But, someone may say to me, are not these Anglican evangelicals still preaching the gospel? The answer is that of course they are. But it seems to me that it is entirely nullified and negated by the fact that in this commission and in other places they are acknowledging that the liberal, modernist, almost infidel, attitude to Scripture and interpretation of Scripture is a possible point of view and a possible interpretation. So what they say on the one hand is negated by what they say on the other hand. They have also changed their view of bishops and their view on the sacraments and on many other subjects.

But still more striking is their change on the matter of *ecclesiastical relationships*. Until comparatively recently, these Anglican evangelicals would have nothing to do with the World Council of Churches. In addition, they claimed that the Anglican Church belonged to them. In the Evangelical Alliance, they put forward the policy of a benevolent neutrality. But, in the Keele Conference of 1967, they openly stated that they had been wrong in their view of others in the church and that they repented of it. In future their attitude was going to be entirely different. They were no longer going to stand on the sidelines, as it were, but instead would take part fully in the work of the Church of England and in the WCC. That is what they have done and are doing.

Quite recently a letter has been published, signed by 125 prominent Anglican evangelicals. In it they refer to a historic change of stance by evangelicals all over the world in their attitude to Roman Catholics and the Orthodox Church. So they are actually proclaiming and boasting of the fact that their attitude to the Roman Catholic, to the Greek and Russian Orthodox Churches, has undergone an entire change. In the congress held in Nottingham, a leading evangelical actually said in a public meeting that the Protestant Reformation was the greatest tragedy in the history of the church.

We have, you see, this extraordinary change. But, lest you think that this is just a little nonconformist pea-shooting at a great institution, I do not ask you to take my opinion. Let me read you some words by the present Bishop of Leicester, which he has written quite recently. These are his exact words: 'Throughout the first forty or fifty years of my life one was accustomed to a fairly sharp divide between the evangelical and the catholic movements in our church.

Their voting strength in the church assembly could be anticipated fairly accurately. Though held together by a fairly widespread loyalty to the Book of Common Prayer and to the episcopal structure of our church under the state, their emphasis, their language and their programme of services and principles of pastoral care were fairly sharply divided.' But he goes on to say this: 'During these recent years these lines of demarcation have become blurred.' The Bishop of Leicester is a so-called 'broad churchman'. He does not belong to the Anglo-Catholics nor to the evangelical wing, but is in the middle. He says that the differences between the two wings are very much more difficult to define. You see, he finds it difficult to define the difference between an evangelical and an Anglo-Catholic. The Nottingham statement on the whole represents a modern, socially conscious, slightly left-wing approach to many matters. There is to be a Catholic congress held next year and it is clear from the preliminary literature that it is in no sense a direct opposite to what Nottingham stood for. Their arguments lead up to a confident and trustful enthusiasm for the one holy catholic church.

Now there is the evidence. This is what has happened during the past ten years. Some of us were afraid that it might happen in some distant future. It has already taken place, and you have the authority of the Bishop of Leicester for that statement. But not only that. The whole approach has become different. Do you know that at this Anglican conference in Nottingham there was literally no scriptural exposition during the congress? The custom always in evangelical circles was that the first meeting of a conference, as has been here this week, should be exposition of Scripture and of prayer. But there was no such exposition of Scripture in Notttingham. What did they have? Dramatic representation of the Scripture and even dancing. What is more, the type of dancing which went on was described by one of the members of the charismatic movement as a sensual form of dancing. This is modern evangelicalism. You see it represents an entirely new attitude and a new approach. And so it is not surprising that towards the end of that famous congress an intelligent man got up and asked the question: 'What is an evangelical?' He asked for a definition of it. It is not surprising that he had to, in view of what he had seen and heard, is it? It has become very doubtful as to what an evangelical really is. This is a sad, a tragic story. And there are many good, honest men in the Church of England who are filled with grief and sorrow at this. They have expressed their disagreement and their fears. They are very unhappy men. I not only know a number of them, I am praying for them because they are men who want to serve God in a true and in a right manner.

Well now, you may ask me, 'Why has all this happened? What has produced this change? Is there something new? Has there been some new discovery?' The answer is that there is nothing new at all. There has been no new discovery. Well then, you say, why have they undergone this change of position and of attitude to these various matters? To me, there is only one answer. It is that if your doctrine of the church is wrong, eventually you will go wrong everywhere. If you believe in a mixed denomination, one territorial church including everybody, of necessity you have to compromise, and that is precisely what has been taking place. I do not mention the fact that a number of them, I am afraid, have been anxious to have intellectual respectability and to be thought well of by the liberal scholars, so called, and that has animated their action. However, let us grant them that their motives are true; we simply record the tragic fact that there has been such a shift and a change in evangelicalism that an able bishop observer finds it very difficult to draw the line between an evangelical and an Anglo-Catholic.

Very well, what is our task in the light of all this? Our task, my friends, is first and foremost this — *the battle for the Bible*. We are back — and this is the most amazing thing — we are back exactly where our forefathers were 100 years ago. This same fight had to be fought when the higher criticism came into this country from Germany in the 1860s and thereafter. It is the same as the Downgrade Movement that was led by the immortal Charles Haddon Spurgeon. We are back in the same position. Let me prove it to you. I said that what they were concerned about at Nottingham is what is called the new hermeneutic. What does that mean?

Well, here is a description of it. They say the Bible text must first be studied in its original setting with all the resources of honest scholarship and then be translated into today's thought. That means much more than finding the equivalent English words for the Hebrew or the Greek and having a translation in English of the Hebrew and the Greek manuscripts. Oh no, you must have much more. You must know the cultural milieu, the cultural setting in which the Scriptures were written, because, and they actually go so far as to say this, you cannot understand the Scriptures unless you know something about this cultural setting. Indeed, one of the leaders of this school on the continent of Europe has actually said that it is virtually impossible for any man to understand even the New Testament today because we can never put ourselves into the cultural position and the thought forms of the people of the first century.

Now this is their new attitude, you see, towards the Scripture. This new hermeneutic was taught from the platform at the congress at Nottingham. It was neither disputed nor denied by any one of the leaders. It is apparently the accepted teaching. You cannot understand the Scriptures though you have them in English. You must know first what the scholars know of the cultural background and milieu in which they were written. That is the modern attitude. Need I point out to you the difference between that and what the Reformers called the perspicuity of the Scriptures? Need I tell you what a contrast it presents to what those great men who translated the Scriptures into English in the sixteenth century believed when they said that we must have the Scriptures in a language 'understood of the people'. No, no, that is no longer enough. Poor old Tyndale and others who looked forward with such glee and delight to the ploughboy and others reading their Scriptures in the fields and rejoicing in the knowledge of the Word of God! How ridiculous all that was, these men say. What does the ploughboy know of the cultural medium, the cultural background? My friends, this is a departure from the view of the Bible which the Reformers held and which their descendants have held until comparatively recently. It is a denial of the essential evangelical position.

But what else are we fighting for? Well, we are fighting for *the truth of the gospel*. This is being compromised by these people. How? Well, by their associations. Did you know that these evangelicals are meeting in committee with all kinds of people, including the Roman Catholics, to prepare for an evangelistic campaign? The Roman Catholics are to be a part of this joint evangelistic effort, presenting the gospel to the people of this country. They have already had what they called the Call to the North and the Roman Catholics were involved in that. And even here in Islington, an evangelical vicar has been co-operating with Roman Catholics in distributing copies of the Gospel of St Mark in all the households in that area. It is not enough to say, 'Ah, but these men are still preaching the gospel.' Very well, let me grant that they are preaching the gospel, but if they say that they are ready to co-operate with the Roman Catholics and their view of salvation, they are denying what they themselves are uttering. So the gospel is being compromised. Do you believe in baptismal regeneration? Well, if you do, what is the point of evangelism?

But we are also fighting a battle for the church, for *a true conception of the Christian church*. We, who belong to the BEC, are not interested in the ecclesiastical politics. We do not go around saying that we have got the ball at our feet and we are going to be the controlling party in a mixed denomination. We are not interested in positions and power. We are not content to be an evangelical wing in a mixed community. We are not prepared to recognize as Christians all who call themselves by that name. This is what these people are doing. They assume that if a man says, 'I am a Christian,' and he belongs to a church, it does not matter what he believes, it does not matter what he denies; if he regards himself as a Christian, they regard him as a Christian. And they say that it is wrong on our part to say that any man is not a Christian if he says that he is.

Furthermore, we are quite clear about the importance of the purity of the church. We are separatists. We are nonconformists. We are dissenters. We do not believe that the institution comes first and that it must be preserved, even at the expense of tolerating denials of essential truth. We believe in the purity of the Word preached and in the regular administration of the sacraments. And we believe in discipline in those respects at the same time.

Indeed, I can summarize our attitude on this question of our view of the church in some words that were spoken by the great Chatham, William Pitt the Elder. He seems to me to have stated our position very perfectly in the House of Lords in 1773 when he was replying to some rather rude remarks that had been made by the then Archbishop of Canterbury about dissenting ministers.

This is what Chatham said: 'The dissenting minsters are represented as men of close ambition. They are so, my lords. And their ambition is to keep close to the college of fishermen, not of cardinals. And to the doctrines of inspired apostles, not to the decrees of interested and aspiring bishops. They contend for a scriptural and spiritual worship.' That is what the dissenters contend for — a scriptural and a spiritual worship. 'We', said Chatham, speaking as a nominal Anglican, 'we have a Calvinistic creed, a popish liturgy and Arminian clergy.' And what he said in 1773 is equally true in 1977.

Or if you prefer someone a litle bit nearer to us than the great Lord Chatham, take what was said by a Puritan member of Parliament in the House of Commons in 1643. 'Take heed', he said, 'of building on an old frame that must be plucked down to the ground. Take heed of plastering when you should be pulling down.' We are not interested in plastering the cracks. We are not interested in reading out a joint statement, nor in the subtleties which emphasize the difference between a joint statement and an agreed statement. We are not interested in this kind of jesuitry. When we hear that a man is going to read out a joint statement, we assume that it is going to be a statement about which they are all agreed. They are jointly agreed. Ah, but they tell us, this is only a joint statement. It is not an agreed statement. They are simply papering over the cracks and presenting a façade of unanimity which hides much difference and disagreement behind the scenes. We are not interested in plastering when we should be pulling down. A mixed denomination must of necessity go astray. You compromise the moment you set it up as an ideal. And the last ten years have given us this tragic evidence of what inevitably takes place.

Very well, there is the general strategy. Shall I mention the particular tactical points I think we ought to remember? First, *we must always pay attention to principles, not to personalities*. We are being told so regularly, 'I cannot believe that so-and-so can subscribe to that. He is such a nice man, such a good man, even a pious man.' That is the argument. I even heard people using it about the late Pope John XXIII. They said he looked such a nice and loving old man. They seemed to have gone more than halfway already to accepting his doctrine simply because he looked a nice man. My dear friends, our Lord warns us against wolves in sheep's clothing. Because a man is nice and good does not guarantee that what he teaches is of necessity right.

The second point that I would establish is that you must not judge only on what men wrote ten or twelve or fifteen years ago. *You must take what they are writing now*. They may have been perfectly all right fifteen years ago. That does not guarantee that they are still right. Men can change.

Another point that I would make is this: *you must take all that a man writes*. You must not merely take some of his books, or one of his books. You must look at all of his books. Why do I say that? Well, I say it for this reason. Take this excitement recently about this book bearing the title of *The Myth of God Incarnate*. Suddenly, evangelical people are comforted and cheered. Ah, they say, it is all right. An Anglican evangelical has edited a reply to that, bearing the title *The Truth of God Incarnate*. How wonderful! I am going to mention his name because he took it upon himself to mention my name in an article in a book which was published earlier this year called *The people of God*. It was one of the preparatory books for the Nottingham Conference. I am referring to Canon Michael Green of St Aldate's Church in Oxford. Ah, they say, is this not wonderful? Here is Michael Green answering these infidels who have written *The Myth of God Incarnate*. Who were the contributors to *The Myth of God Incarnate*? Well, one of the most prominent was Professor Maurice Wiles of Oxford. And Michael Green denounces his ideas, his views of the person of our Lord. Well, you say, wonderful!

Yes, but you know, you must look at other statements to which he has contributed and here is one of them. In this book called *Christian Believing* the first section was agreed by all the members of the commission. Among them was Michael Green, and this is what he subscribes to: 'It is tempting in the weariness and distress of conflict between followers of a common Lord [Maurice Wiles, who does not believe in the deity of Christ, is referred to here as one who is a follower of a common Lord] to opt for a radical and simplistic solution by which a decision is taken to rule out one or more of these competing attitudes. But we are convinced that any such decision would be disastrous to the health of the church. The tension must be endured. What is important is that everything should be done to make it a creative tension. That is not a state of long communication between mutually embattled groups but one of constant dialogue with consequent cross-fertilization of ideas and insights. The quality of this dialogue is determined by three inseparable factors. First, it takes place within the community of faith. [They are all members of the Church of England, you see, and therefore of the community of faith.] It is not simply an intellectual debate, but an unceasing effort of brothers in Christ.' The Maurice Wiles who is denounced with the others who in *The Myth of God Incarnate* deny the incarnation, the virgin birth, the supernatural, the miraculous, the atoning death, the literal physical resurrection and the person of the Holy Spirit, the man whom Michael Green denounces in one book, is referred to as a brother in Christ in this other book.

So, my dear friends, you must not merely look at one book that is written by such men or a contribution to one book. You must take everything that they write.

And lastly, you must not only note what they say and what they write, but also what they do. This is important for this reason that they say in their declaration that they are going to hold out to us the right hand of fellowship — I rather think it is the left, but they say it is the right, the right hand of fellowship. My reply to that is that no interpretation of Matthew 6:3 covers this. What is Matthew 6:3? It is: 'When thou doest thine alms let not thy left hand know what thy right hand doeth.' I am afraid that we have got to watch both hands. Though one hand is held out to us, we must notice that the other hand is held out to the Roman Catholics. And so we are brought together, willy nilly. I, for one, say it is impossible. We cannot be a part of this. These men's actions are as important as their statements and as their writings. Well, there is the sword and the battle.

The song

Let me say a hurried word about the other aspect: 'Let the high praises of God be in their mouth.' We have got to fight — unfortunately, but we must fight for the truth, for the Scripture and for the church. We must also fight for the sake of these honest men who are still left behind in some of these bodies and who are unhappy. We can help them. I think they will eventually come to us. They may take time, but they will come. We must also do so for the sake of many Roman Catholics who are utterly bewildered by what is happening in their church. Unless we show them that what we have is entirely different we will not be able to help them. Many of these Roman Catholics, who claim to have had new experiences of the power of the Holy Ghost, say that there is no need for them to leave their church because if they were to go to other churches they would simply find what they have already got. We can help these men by showing that a true view of the Scripture leads to a true view of salvation and to a true view of the church, so that when under the illumination of the Holy Spirit and through reading the Scripture, they see the true position they will turn to us and we will be able to help them and to lead them on.

182 *Unity in truth*

So we must bear this in mind, and in this connection it is essential that we should not only have the sword in our hands, but that we should have the high praises of God in our mouths. We are fighters, yes, but we are not negative; we are not defensive. We are not apologetic. Still less are we frightened. We should not be depressed. We have no business to be mourning in Zion. It is not for us to say, like those poor captives in Babylon who began to hang their harps on the willows, 'How can we sing the Lord's song in a strange land?' Christian people, evangelical people, if we give the impression that we are miserable people, that we are mournful, that we are just negative critics — well, we do not deserve to be noticed. But we are not to be that. We are not in the strange land. We are no longer in Babylon. We were once there, but as a remnant we have come back to Jerusalem. So we no longer can ask the question: 'How can we sing the Lord's song in a strange land?' We are back, I say, in Jerusalem. And we are not to weep. The word that comes to us is the word that Nehemiah and Ezra delivered, you remember, to that handful of people who went back to reconstruct and to re-establish Jerusalem. They were told: 'Mourn not, nor weep, for the joy of the Lord is your strength.'

'The high praises of God in the mouth.' Though a remnant, weak and small, it does not matter. Wield the sword, but above all sing the high praises of the Lord. This is the exhortation of the Bible everywhere from beginning to end. 'The sword of the Lord and of Gideon.' You remember the capture of Jericho, the great city of Jericho. How did that come to the ground? It was as the result of a shout of the people of God. They were commanded to give a great shout, and when they did the walls of the city fell flat. Of course, we are persecuted, but remember the words of our Lord: 'Blessed are ye, when men shall revile you, and persecute you, and say all manner of evil against you.' 'Rejoice', he says, be glad because of this, because 'great is your reward in heaven.' We are blessed; we should be exceeding glad.

What was the condition of the early church? How small they were in number, with everything against them! They seemed utterly insignificant, but you remember what we are told about that church at the end of Acts 2. It is what should be true of us: 'And they, continuing daily with one accord in the temple, and breaking bread from house to house, did eat their meat with gladness and singleness of heart, praising God.' Are we praising God? How are we to attract people if we are mournful and unhappy, morbid and introspective and groaning and moaning? No, no, we are to praise the Lord who is God. The high praises of God should be on our lips. And do you remember that, even when they were threatened and beaten, and being put to death was not impossible, we are told that they departed from the presence of the council, rejoicing that they were counted worthy to suffer shame for his sake? That is to be our condition.

Do you remember the story of Paul and Silas in the prison? Arrested, backs scourged, beaten, feet fast in the stocks, everything against them. But this is what I read: 'At midnight Paul and Silas prayed and sang praises unto God.' Are we doing this? Are we giving people the impression that, because we have the truth of God and believe it as it is, we are a rejoicing people? That is the way to attract people and it is something which we are commanded to do.

You remember one of the last injunctions of the apostle Paul in his letter to the church at Philippi. He says, 'Rejoice in the Lord always, and again, I say, rejoice.' But, you say, how can you rejoice when you are being persecuted? How can you rejoice when you are but a small company of people and the big battalions are on the other side, when you may be persecuted and everything is against you and you are getting no results? Well, the apostle does not tell us to re-joice in the lack of results nor to rejoice in any one of the other things. He says, 'Rejoice in the Lord.' And this is something that we can always do and we must do. I believe this is the greatest challenge that comes to us as constituent members of this BEC. We are standing for the truth. We are fighting for the truth. But are we rejoicing in it? Are we such people as these early Christians were? That is what makes people long for what we have: the high praises of God in our hearts and on our lips, living to his praise and to his glory!

How can you do this when everything is against you? The answer is quite simple. You rejoice in the Lord; you praise him because he is who and what he is. 'Praise the Lord, ye heavens, adore him. Praise him, angels in the height.' If we really believe what we read about him, we must praise him. We are not here to defend him, but to praise him and to show that we have a knowledge *of* him and not merely a knowledge *about* him.

His high praises should be on our lips because of what he has done in his Son. He has visited and redeemed his people. He has sent his only Son into the world as the Redeemer and as the Saviour. We must praise him. Whatever may be happening to us, we do not wait for the mood or the state, we do not even wait for results. We praise him for what he has done, for the wonderful works of God.

The high praises of God should be upon our lips for what he has done in us. We are no longer 'miserable offenders'. That is the Prayer Book. What are we? We are sons of God. We are the children of the living God. The exhortation that comes to us is this:

Children of the heavenly King,
As ye journey, sweetly sing.

Are you singing? I am not asking for something artificial. I am asking for such a realization of the truth of salvation and our experience of it that we must sing, because we are children of the heavenly King and because we are marching to Zion. Praise him for what you have already got, for what you have already experienced of his exceeding great and precious promises. Praise him for what you already are. What are you? I am what I am by the grace of God. I am no longer in Adam. I am in Christ. Praise him for that. It does not matter what is happening round and about you; we should be praising him every time we meet together. We meet together on Sundays to worship God. Do you praise him? Are you rejoicing in him? Are you telling forth the wonders of his grace in general and in particular?

We should praise him, not only because of what we already are and what he has already done for us; we should praise him because we know that in our warfare he has told us that he will never leave us nor forsake us. And beyond it all, we should praise him as we look forward and have an occasional glimpse of that inheritance incorruptible and undefiled and that fadeth not away, reserved in heaven by God for us. Oh, yes, we shall see him. We shall see him in the flesh. The body is going to be raised. It is not merely a continuation of existence; it is a redemption of the entire man, body, soul and spirit. We shall see him as he is, and we shall be made like unto him in the glory everlasting. He will change this body of our humiliation and fashion it like unto the body of his glorification, according to the mighty working whereby he is able even to subdue all things unto himself. We with the apostles must say, 'We ought to obey God rather than men,' and even sing it.

Well, that, my friends, seems to me to be the call that comes to us in the BEC at this present moment. It is a tragic story that I have had to remind you of, but they are facts. Take up the sword, use it. Familiarize yourselves with what is happening. You find the books I have referred to reviewed in the *Evangelical Times*. Buy the books if you can and read them. Support your ministers. Get them to tell you about the contents of these books. You are all in the conflict. It is not a battle for ministers alone. We are all in it together. And we must fight the battle of the Lord together. And above all, I say, his high praises should be in our hearts, in our mouths and on our lips. What a God we have to praise! And how we should thank him that he has ever been pleased to look upon us, even us, and to open our eyes to the wonders of his grace, giving us an occasional glimpse of that state in which, when this poor, stammering tongue lies rotting in the grave, we shall join the everlasting choir in singing the song of Moses and the Lamb. May God enable us to do so to the glory of his great and holy name. Amen.

10.
Render unto Cæsar

The Doctor's last address at a BEC conference was given at Westminster Chapel on 7 November 1979. In it he dealt with the subject of the relation between the Christian, and the Christian church, and social concerns and the state. This had become a matter of growing importance to evangelicals at large and since then it has assumed even greater prominence. What he had to say stressed the priority of the spiritual and the eternal and the necessity of praying for an outpouring of the Spirit of God.

I would like to say briefly how very privileged I am to be here once more in the final rally of the British Evangelical Council meeting here in Westminster Chapel, London. I have always regarded it as a very great honour to speak at this conference.

I want to call your attention to one of the paragraphs from the 22nd chapter of the Gospel according to St Matthew, namely verses 15 to 22 inclusive. Let me remind you of them: 'Then went the Pharisees, and took counsel how they might entangle him in his talk. And they sent out unto him their disciples with the Herodians, saying, Master, we know that thou art true, and teachest the way of God in truth, neither carest thou for any man: for thou regardest not the person of men. Tell us therefore, What thinkest thou? Is it lawful to give tribute to Cæsar, or not? But Jesus perceived their wickedness, and said, Why tempt ye me, ye hypocrites? Show me the tribute money. And they brought unto him a penny. And he saith unto them, Whose is this image and superscription? They say unto him, Cæsar's. Then saith he unto them, Render therefore unto Cæsar the things which are Cæsar's; and unto God the things that are

God's. When they had heard these words, they marvelled, and left him and went their way.'

You will recall from your familiarity with the Scriptures that this was the first of a series of deputations that waited upon the Lord Jesus Christ and put their varying questions to him. Now I always feel, whenever I read this particular chapter, that it puts before us, in a most extraordinary and dramatic manner, the great tragedy, indeed *the* greatest tragedy of mankind. Here, you see, we have a picture of a world that was in trouble. Anyone who is familiar with the secular history of the world at the time when these things took place will know that it was a world that was full of trouble and full of problems. Well, into such a world the Lord Jesus Christ came, the only person who could solve its problems. Yet what we find here, as indeed in all the Gospels, is a world refusing to listen to him, a world rejecting him. We read of these people that 'They marvelled', but though they marvelled, 'They left Jesus and went their way.'

Now that, I say, is a picture of the real, essential tragedy in the life of mankind and of the human race. In a word, it refuses to listen to the only one who could really help. The Bible, which is the record of God's great purpose of salvation, is at the same time a record of the follies of mankind in resisting God's plan and God's way. So what we have here in miniature is the message of the entire Bible. I am calling your attention to this particular matter because it seems to me that it immediately brings us face to face with the greatest tragedy of our modern world. Here we are once more, meeting in a world of mounting crisis, of increasing difficulties and problems. And yet, as in the first century, what is happening in the world is that men and women are prepared to listen to almost anything except to the message concerning this blessed person.

So it behoves us, in the BEC, to consider this question together: what can we do in the light of this indifference? What is the business of the Christian church at a time such as this? What is our duty as individual Christians when we talk with men and women about their problems, perplexities and the whole state of the world at this critical hour? What I want to try to show you is that if we really want to be effective we must follow the example of our blessed Lord as he dealt with those people who came to him. Let me show you from this portion of Holy Scripture what is involved in that by means of certain lessons which we badly need to learn as churches and as individual Christians.

A wrong approach

The first thing can be pointed up by means of the following
questions. Why was it that these people behaved in this manner
towards our Lord? Or, why was it that the Son of God was ever
rejected and despised and died on a cruel cross? What is the cause
of this? Why is the world today refusing to listen to his message? The
simple answer to these questions can be put in this form: their whole
approach to Jesus was entirely wrong. You know, the difficulty with
people who reject the gospel and who are not Christians is never
really with regard to any of the particular details of Christianity.
They like to think that it is, but that is not really the fundamental
problem. The particular difficulties arise because their entire approach is wrong.

That is something that comes out very clearly here in the case of
these Pharisees and Herodians who went to him as a deputation on
this occasion. What do we find about them? Well, what is so
noticeable is that they were trying to be clever. *They were trying to
catch him.* You see, they agreed to say together when they went to
him, 'Master, we know that thou art true and teachest the way of God
in truth, neither carest thou for any man ...' and so on. 'Tell us,
therefore, what thinkest thou? Is it lawful to give tribute unto Cæsar
or not?' You see, they were deliberately trying to trip him and to
catch him. Their country had been conquered by the Romans, who
had imposed their laws and taxes upon them. Whether the Jews
should pay these taxes was therefore a burning political question at
the time. Now they were perfectly aware that whichever answer our
Lord gave to that question, he would get himself into trouble. That
was what they wanted and so they framed their question accord-
ingly. Of course, they went and paid him their compliments, as many
people still do who pay compliments to 'Jesus', as they call him, and
to his teaching. They expressed interest or appreciation, but it was
all hypocrisy. Their real object was to show their cleverness and to
trap him.

I think you will often find in discussions with people about the
Christian faith, and many other matters, that men and women really
do not want to find the truth. They are out to show their cleverness
and they have their famous catch questions. We are all familiar with
them: 'Who was Cain's wife?' 'What was that creature that swal-
lowed Jonah?' You are familiar with all the old chestnuts, the catch

questions about how can there be a God when such terrible things as poliomyelitis and various other tragic physical conditions occur in the lives of men and women? Now this is the first thing about those people. They were not serious. They were more concerned about their cleverness and their trick questions than they really were to arrive at a knowledge of the truth. So are our contemporaries.

The next thing to note is that *they are governed by their prejudices and by their own ideas*. Do you notice what the different deputations say? They all have different interests and each one comes with that which is uppermost in its mind and creed. In other words, they did not have open minds. They had their prejudices, their preconceived ideas, and they were more concerned about those than they were about a knowledge of the truth itself.

But, so that I can finish this bit of analysis which is more or less psychological, the real trouble with these people can be put in this form: these foolish people did all the talking instead of listening. Now I feel this is something we must assert to the modern world. You remember what happened when the apostle Paul visited Athens for the first time. There he was confronted by Stoics and Epicureans, philosophers — very clever people who spent their time in talking, arguing and debating, and so on. And that is what they were beginning to do with Paul. But you remember what the apostle Paul said to them: 'Whom ye ignorantly worship, him declare I unto you.' My friends, your business and mine as Christian people is to declare to people. We must get them to see that all their talk ends where it began and if they really want help, then they must learn to listen. Have you noticed how often in discussions about these matters over the media people who have obviously never read their Bibles express their opinions freely and confidently? They are simply expressing their prejudices and their philosophies. And the church can only have an impact on the world once more if she has the boldness, the authority, to call upon men and women to be silent and to listen to the truth which she has to declare.

An over-preoccupation with lesser things

Let me move on to the second lesson which is equally clear from this passage. It follows directly from the first. It is a part of our business to show our contemporaries that they are over-preoccupied with the

lesser things in life. Notice, I am not saying that they are preoccupied
with things that are of no account whatsoever. I am saying that they
are preoccupied with things that are of *comparatively less importance*. I hope no one will go away with the impression that I am
saying that the things people are preoccupied with are of no
importance whatsoever. That is not the case. What happens is that
they give them an order of importance which they do not merit. Now
look at these people here. They were concerned about this question
of paying taxes to Cæsar, to the Roman Empire.

You find in the world today that men and women come to us as
the church, or as individual Christians, wanting to discuss with us
particular questions that are of interest to them. What are they? I
think if you are at all aware of what is happening in the world today
you will find that its questions are very similar to those of the first
century. Their concerns are social and political. We must be alert
here because a new tendency is coming in even amongst
evangelicals. It is to be thinking and talking increasingly about
social and political questions. You are aware that in South America
and in other parts of the world they are very interested in what they
call the 'Theology of Liberation', or 'Liberation Theology'. You are
probably familiar that in all the great congresses of the so-called
'World Church', those are the matters that they are discussing.
Many are saying that it is the business of the Christian church to lead
the world revolution, to mitigate suffering and to right wrongs, to
bring in social justice. Then there are others who put their whole
emphasis upon knowledge and culture. These are not so much
interested in the political aspect but in art and drama instead and
everything that belongs to the realm of culture. This again has
become increasingly popular among us. Well, they were doing it in
the first century, and they are still doing it today. There are those who
are interested in literature, and so on. I do not want to weary you with
the list.

How should we respond to this? The first thing to say is that these
things are all perfectly legitimate. It is a fallacy to say that the
Christian is to have no interest in politics or in social affairs. That is
not a true part of the Christian tradition nor the tradition of the church
at her best. We are all to be citizens in this world. Our Lord made this
clear by saying what his questioners did not expect, namely,
'Render unto Cæsar those things that are Cæsar's.' He told them to

pay their taxes. So we must say that it is the business of Christians to behave as citizens in the world, to feel a sense of responsibility for what is happening and to do what they can or are called to do in local, national or even international politics. There must be no question about all this at all. The same applies to art and literature. The Christian is not some philistine. He is not some kind of boorish person. I am afraid we have often given this impression and we have therefore antagonized people. But that is not true to our scriptural teaching. We believe that all these gifts that are exercised in art and culture and in various other respects have been given by God to men, and we are meant to use them. There is such a thing as common grace, and it is not part of the preaching of the gospel to say that the Christian is to take no interest whatsoever in these various aspects of life. They are all perfectly legitimate.

But what is emphasized in our paragraph is that we must not be obsessed by these things. The trouble with these people was that they had but one interest, this question of the taxes, just as others had their little question about the resurrection and so on. What comes out so clearly here is that these people thought of nothing else. This seems to be the whole of life to them.

Now, our Lord deals with that, and I am here to suggest that we must too by putting these things into the right place and into the right proportion. We must not give them an order of importance which they do not merit. We must not be over-preoccupied with them. So we must answer as our Lord does. We must say, 'Yes, render unto Cæsar the things that are Cæsar's.' In their place, it is all right to be talking about politics, if you like, and social matters, and art and culture and drama, but they must not be in the centre. You must not be over-preoccupied with them. That is one of the dangerous tendencies that I observe. Anyone who follows at all what happens at meetings of the so-called World Council of Churches will know that very often the entire time is given over to this. More and more evangelicals, as well as others, are putting these things into the centre and everybody is talking about the Christian attitude to politics, or education, or culture, or war, or this or that. This has become central. Our Lord's teaching is, 'No, no! Render unto Cæsar the things that are Cæsar's.' It is all right to take an interest in these things, but do not be obsessed by them. Do not put them into the centre of the picture. Do not be always talking about them. If we do, the impression will be gained that Christianity is nothing but some kind of exceptional or strange philosophical attitude towards a number of burning contemporary social questions.

To conclude this point, let me put the matter like this: the church is not to allow her task and function to be governed by the questions of people. This contradicts what we are being told today, does it not? We are told that people today are not interested in preaching. They are not interested much in Christianity directly. They have no interest at all in theology. Therefore, the church's business, we are told, is to find out what they are interested in. What is your neighbour interested in? Is it politics? Well, go and discuss politics with him. Show him the inadequacy of his politics and instead what you call 'Christian politics'. Or, if your neighbour is interested in art, well, go and talk to him about art and show him the inadequacies of his secular conception of art. Then, give him the great contrast of Christian art. And so with drama, with novels, with literature, and with everything.

That seems to be an exact contradiction of what our blessed Lord did on this occasion. The whole secret of his replies to these deputations was that he handled their questions in a very light manner — in a sense he dimissed them. He did not allow these matters to be central in his replies. Neither must we. These matters have their place, but they must be kept in their place. And when the church begins to talk about our discovering what the world is interested in and what the world wants to know, she has moved from the position of her blessed Lord and Master.

The task of the church

Very well then, we are to show men and women that they are not to be over-preoccupied with lesser matters. But it does not stop at that, does it? What is the real business of the church? What is the great call to us at the present time? It is to call men and women's attention to the only things that are absolutely essential. Shall I put it to you like this? The great task confronting the church at the moment is to shout one little word. What is it? It is the word 'and'. 'Render unto Cæsar the things that are Cæsar's *and, and,* to God the things that are God's.' This is our calling, my friends. We are not here to discuss art, or literature, or politics, or evolution, or any one of these questions. They have their place, a little apologetic place, but not the central place. No, no! This is where we evangelicals are to come in. This is what we are called to proclaim: 'Render unto Cæsar the things that are Cæsar's *and* ...' that which the world knows nothing about and even the church seems to be forgetting at this time. It is that which is surely at the present time more important perhaps than it has ever been. We are living in a materialistic age. We are living in a sophisticated age. We are living in an age when men and women are experts on all these particular matters. You and I ought to be experts on the things of which they are entirely ignorant. Our supreme calling is to introduce the '*and*', this vital addition.

I want now to put what our Lord includes under this 'and' in the way in which he put it. '*And to God.*' The real tragedy of the world today is that it has forgotten the supernatural. It has forgotten God. Man is in the centre — his interests, his questions, his enthusiasms, his obsessions. Man is ever before us and so our task is to proclaim the everlasting and eternal God. And we must do this in the way that our Lord himself did on this very interesting occasion. Let me remind you how he brought out this truth. It was by means of a contrast. He said, in reply to their question, 'Render therefore unto Cæsar the things that are Cæsar's and unto God the things that are God's.' There is a contrast here, is there not? Let me show you something of its nature. It has three parts.

The things themselves

First of all, it contains a contrast between two sets of things — between 'the things' that are Cæsar's and 'the things' that are God's. That is the contrast that our Lord put before these people when he adopted this peculiar illustration and device. When they put their question to him and he perceived their wickedness, he asked them to show him the tribute money. Drawing their attention to the coin, he asked them, 'Whose is this image and superscription?' 'Cæsar's' they replied. He then told them to give to Cæsar what belonged to him. The coin represented that category of things.

Let us therefore look at the matter in that way. There are things that belong to Cæsar, just as there are things that belong to God. Now the things that are Cæsar's can be summed up, if you like, by referring to Cæsar's image — it is the world's view of man himself.

Because the world thinks of man in this materialistic age in terms of things, man is himself regarded as a bundle of sensations. According to some learned authorities, man is nothing but chemistry and physics. Others regard man as a purely political animal. Still others regard him as an economic unit. As you know full well, these are the terms which are current at the present time. Man is regarded as someone who works to get money and, having got money, he eats and drinks and indulges in sex, and so on. That is the view of man prevalent at the present time. Man is regarded as some kind of highly developed technological instrument. And so, the whole view of man and of life is one that thinks in these materialistic terms — this coin and what it can buy for me in the way of material gains. That is the modern position with regard to the things that are Cæsar's.

But wait a moment, and this is where our Lord brought in his message to them. Visualize him, looking at the coin and saying, 'Tell me, whose is this image and superscription?' And they say unto him 'Cæsar's.' 'Very well,' he says, 'Give those things to Cæsar. Give politics; give the social interests, money, taxes — all the things that belong to that secular realm, give them to the secular realm and to Cæsar. That is where they belong.' And then, I believe, he lifted up his head and he questioned them with his eyes. Having asked, 'Whose is this image and superscription?' he looked into their eyes and in effect said, 'Whose image is on you?'

In that way he introduced his teaching with regard to man which is the whole Christian biblical view. What is man? Ignorance on this point is the great tragedy of the age, is it not? Man, as I say, has been regarded as a mere speck in the universe. The individual is increasingly being forgotten altogether in the mass of humanity. The modern view of man is so debased and you and I, my friends, are to tell men and women that it is an insult to man. What is man? He is a creature, created in the image and the likeness of God. Man is not an animal. He is not here just to make money and have motor cars and to have the finest food and drink and sex. No, no! Man was made in the image and likeness of God. He was made to be a companion of God. He was meant for fellowship with God. He does not belong to this realm of things. He uses them and they have their place. They are essential to life, but that is not man. He does not give himself to these things. So we must proclaim this great truth that man is a living soul, that he has within him what is greater than the whole world itself, something that is greater than all our definitions and all our understanding. Listen! This is the kind of thing we are to say in the words of a poet:

Tell me not in mournful numbers,
Life is but an empty dream,
For the soul is dead that slumbers,
And things are not what they seem.
Life is real, life is earnest,
And the grave is not its goal,
Dust thou art, to dust returnest
Was not spoken of the soul.

But men and women have no conception of the soul. They think that they are just animals whose cerebrum has developed a little more than that of the average animal, and they never speak about a soul, this amazing quality within us that makes us capable of communion with the everlasting and eternal God. Or, as our Lord put it differently on another occasion, when he was preaching and saying some of the most amazing things that he ever said, it seems that he paused to take breath, and immediately, a fellow in the crowd shouted out. 'Master,' he said, 'speak to my brother, that he divide the inheritance with me.' Our Lord looked at the man, amazed and shocked, and said, 'Who made me a judge or a ruler over you?' Then he went on to utter these words: 'A man's life [his soul] consisteth not in the abundance of things that he possesseth.' But that was that man's view of man. He thought of himself in terms of possessions and he was obsessed by this idea.

Or, yet again, listen to our Lord: 'Man does not live by bread alone.' All this thirst for more money — and it runs right through society, not only the trade unions, but also the capitalist — everybody wants more money. The answer to it all is that man is a living soul and does not live by bread alone.

But finally, 'What shall it profit a man though he gain the whole world and lose his own soul?' This soul — this amazing thing that God has made us, which differentiates us from all the animals and from all creation and which makes man the lord of creation. Whose is that image and superscription? Whose image and superscription is on you? We are to tell men and women, and it is the thing they need to be told above everything else, that their dignity and greatness, above and beyond the whole world, is the consequence of their having been made by God and for God and nothing can finally satisfy them except God.

The owners of the things

But look for a moment with me at the second contrast which is drawn here by our Lord. It concerns the owners, or the controllers, of the things referred to. 'Render unto Cæsar the things that are Cæsar's ... Render unto God the things that are God's.' He tells them to pay tribute to Cæsar. Why? Because Cæsar has authority and power. Cæsar is the great Roman Emperor and he is the highest member in the seat of government. He is not therefore to be trifled with, because after all, Cæsar has considerable power. If you disobey Cæsar you will be punished. Cæsar controls the legislature, he passes the acts of parliament to control our lives and if you break the laws you will be arraigned in court, you can be punished, fined, thrown into prison. He can even take your life from you. So you must pay your taxes to Cæsar. You cannot contract out of life. Many are trying to do it today but they will always end in trouble. Cæsar is to be obeyed because he exercises great authority and great power. I think we are going to see more and more of this in our modern world. This is an acute problem for many of our brethren in lands behind the so-called 'Iron Curtain' and it is important that they should realize these things. Cæsar is not to be despised. Cæsar has great power. Therefore pay your tribute to Cæsar.

But while we must be obedient, law-abiding citizens, and indeed be an example of that to everybody else, we do not stop at that. Why? Well, because there is a limit to what Cæsar can claim and do. We must preach that. The great Cæsars, the great dictators — there is a limit to their authority and power. As I have told you, they can do many things to us, but thank God there are some things that they cannot do. They can throw us into prison, but they cannot stop us thinking. They cannot stop us loving; they cannot stop us imagining. They cannot touch us there. And after all, your great Cæsars are but mortal men. 'Princes and lords may flourish or may fade, a breath can make them as a breath has made.' The greatest Cæsar, the greatest dictator, must needs get old and die and his authority ends. But quite apart from that, Cæsar, in his might and authority, as I say, can even put you to death, but when he has done so he can do no more.

Do you remember our Lord told that to his timorous disciples as he sent them out to preach on one occasion? They were very afraid of persecutions and what men and women would do to them, and he said to them, 'My friends, fear not them that kill the body, and after that have no more that they can do, but I will forewarn you whom you must fear. Fear him who having killed the body hath power to cast into hell.' So you render unto Cæsar because of his authority and power, but you see the limit to his power. And then, our Lord says positively, 'Render unto God the things that are God's.' Why? Because God is God.

This is something that the modern world knows nothing about. They talk about God, but it is a figment of their own own thinking and their own imaginings. They know nothing of the God who has revealed himself uniquely in the person of his only begotten Son. Who is he? He is not a man. He is the great Jehovah — the I AM. He is the one without beginning and without end, the Creator of the ends of the earth. He is the artificer, the sustainer of everything that is. He is the everlasting God. He is the God who has made us all. He is the one who has made even the Cæsars. He is the God in whose hand our breath is, and all our ways. He controls everything. Nothing is beyond him. 'Wide as the world is thy command' we sang at the beginning, 'Wide is the world at thy command,' cannot be said of any Cæsar. 'Vast as eternity is thy love.' This is only true of God, the illimitable, the all-powerful, the everlasting and eternal God. And, my dear friends, we are all in his hands. You have no idea as to whether you are going to be alive tomorrow morning or not. Not one of us knows. 'Our times are in his hands.'

And not only that, look at the world we are living in at the present time. Look at its mounting problems; look at the gathering clouds. People are concerned about it, and rightly so. But do they think at all about life in its ultimate sense? We are all getting older. I am reminded of that every time I stand in this pulpit. It is all right, my friends, it is true of you as well! You will soon be as old as I am. We are all getting older. We have all got to die and after death, judgement. Now this is what the world knows nothing about. It never thinks about it at all. It knows a great deal about the power of Cæsar, but the troubles in our world tonight are due to the fact that men and women are ignorant of the power of God. The power of God is the power of our Maker, the power of our Judge eternal and we are all moving, as is the whole cosmos, in the direction of a final assize,

a last judgement. And as our Lord reminded his disciples on that
occasion, our destiny is in the hands of God. He has power, after we
have died, not only to judge us, but if we have disobeyed him and
refused him, to cast us to everlasting and eternal punishment. I am
not saying this; it is the Lord Jesus Christ who talked about the place
where 'The worm dieth not and the fire is not quenched.' My dear
friends, do you and I, as Christians, do we contemplate as we ought
to do the power of the everlasting and eternal God? We should be
humbled under his almighty hand and serve him with reverence and
godly fear, not dance and joke and merely sing before him, but serve
him with reverence and godly fear. Why? 'For our God is a
consuming fire!' That is the second contrast.

The benefits

Let me just say a word about the third and the last contrast. This is,
of course, the contrast between the benefits that the two powers can
give us. Are you paying your taxes? Well, you pay taxes because you
get certain benefits from the state and from the government, and let
us not despise them. The state can do many things for us, and that
is why we should be ready always, and pleased to pay our rates and
taxes. It can give us wages and pensions, education and technology;
it can give us housing; it can look after our health; it can provide
pleasure for us and protect us up to a point. These are the benefits that
the state can and does give us. And we should be grateful for these
and not despise them.

But, my dear friends, there is a very great limit to what the state
can do for any one of us. In spite of all that the state provides, it
cannot give us the most precious things in the world. What are they?
Here is one of them. What do you do with your own solitude? What
do you do when you meet disappointment in life? What can the state
do for you when you are let down by some trusted friend? What has
the world at its best and highest, not only its government but also its
culture, to give to man when all his brightest dreams are withering
and dying at his feet? What can the state and culture do for misery
and unhappiness and loneliness? What has it got to give us when we
are lying on our deathbeds? Now this is one of the most hopeful
features that I am aware of at the present time, that even the secular

world is beginning to see the limits of what the state, what Cæsar can do for us.

Let me read you one or two statements to that effect. Here is a statement by the President of the British Society for Social Responsibility and Science: 'To say that science has value because its application can bring a man great benefits is true, but it is not enough. The benefits are largely material, such as improving the standard of living or conquering diseases. These are of the highest priority in backward countries but in technologically advanced countries need for material advance is much less urgent. And young people especially tend to turn their backs on such material concerns. They express more interest in the quality of life in terms of spiritual values and human relationships.' And is that not true?

Or take a statement I read last year by the wife of a great scientist, a scientist herself. She wrote, 'At last we are beginning to realize the worst.' 'And what is that?' we may ask. It is that 'No scientific or technological trick is going to improve the quality of life.' Men and women are at last awakening to this: the quality of life. A big bank balance does not guarantee happiness. Some of the most wretched poeple in the earth are multi-millionaires. No, no! The things that are of greatest value in life — peace of conscience, tranquillity in heart, happiness and joy — this world cannot give. Indeed your culture cannot. I read recently a statement by Lord Clarke, our leading authority on culture. He and another man were having a discussion together about a great artist who had died. And Lord Clarke, the man who propagates the notion of culture so much, he actually said this: 'Lives devoted to beauty usually end badly.' That is the question, you see: how am I to live? How am I to die? How am I to face the unknown eternity? And at that point Cæsar, politics, culture — everything that the world prizes most of all has simply nothing whatsoever to give us.

Thank God, we can turn to the contrary. Look at the benefits that God gives. What are they? Well, I could keep you to midnight in giving you a mere synopsis of an answer to that question. Here it is in one great verse: 'God so loved the world that he gave his only begotten Son, that whosoever believeth in him should not perish but have everlasting life.' 'What can God give us?' says someone. 'Nobody else seems to be able to give us much.' All the things in which mankind has put its trust are collapsing and failing before our eyes. 'Very well', says someone, 'What can God give me?' I will tell you. God sent his one and only Son into this world. What for? To rescue us out of our lost condition, out of our failure, out of our misery, out of our unhappiness. That is why Christ came into the world, the very Son of God. This is the solution which God gives in the person of his own Son. Not your human solutions, not politics, not philosophy, not culture, but God's own solution, sending his only Son into the world in the likeness of sinful flesh and for sin. And this Son of God of whom we have been reading here in our paragraph, and of whom you can read in the Bible, this Son of God, in order to rescue us and redeem us and to give us glorious benefits, not only lived and endured the contradiction of sinners, not only spent his time working with his holy hands, he even went deliberately to a cruel death upon a cross. What for? To receive from God the punishment of our sins. Why? That we might receive free pardon and forgiveness by God. Is there anything comparable in the universe to this? Though you may have spent all your life to this moment living for self and for the world, and all that goes with it, and though you may have sinned even to the very jaws of hell, you have only to believe this message concerning God's way of salvation in his only begotten Son, this Jesus of Nazareth. You have only to believe that your sins were punished in him and they will be forgiven you completely, for he not only bore them and died, but rose again, thereby declaring that God was satisfied, that the penalty had been paid and that God is ready to smile upon us, to forgive us freely and for nothing, without our doing anything, and to begin to shower his blessings upon us.

And what are they? Well, the moment you believe you find that you are a child of God. You are still a man in the world, as he was in the world, but you are a new man. You have been born again, you have got a new nature within you. You know that you are a child of God. You can talk to God as your Father so that 'When all things seem against us, to drive us to despair, we know one gate is open, one ear will hear our prayer.' God becomes a Father to us and he begins to pour his blessings upon us. He will give you peace of conscience. He will give you quiet in your heart. You will be able to put your head on your pillow tonight and sleep like a babe, not fearful of death, or the grave, or of judgement, because you know that you are a child of God. What is more, because you are a child of God, then you are an heir of God himself and a joint heir with Christ.

Oh, the blessings of this Christian life are untold! You have a new outlook upon life and, speaking today, I would particularly emphasize that there is nothing that I know of the Christian life and salvation that is more glorious than the way that it makes you totally independent of circumstances.

The real tragedy of the non-Christian is that he is entirely dependent upon circumstances, and that is why his outlook is very black at the present time. For twenty years he has never had it so good. We are told we are about to enter into not only a deep recession but depression. Your money may cease to come. Suddenly, you will be back in a position of penury — no longer the television, the wireless, the motor car and all the gadgets that science and the state can help you to obtain. You are thrown back on yourself. How are men and women going to live when they have not got so much money that they can buy the best food and drink and have their sex and all their pleasures?

But when you become a Christian you see through all this. You are no longer dependent upon these things. You see through the emptiness of life without God, and dependence upon material things and even upon other people. You are lifted to a new realm; you look at everything from the standpoint of eternity. And what if you should be taken ill, as I have been — and everybody has got to face these things — and be lying alone on a hospital bed, facing a very serious operation in the morning? Your loved ones have gone home, as they must, and you are absolutely alone — there is the test. What are you like then? How do you stand up to solitude? Pascal said on one occasion that the real tragedy of man is that he does not know how to be alone in his own room. How do you contemplate death? How do you contemplate eternity? These are the questions.

Now, the Christian has solved all these questions. He is no longer dependent upon circumstance and chance. He has a well of water within him springing up into everlasting life. He can say with Paul that he is persuaded, he is sure that 'Neither death nor life, nor angels, nor principalities, nor powers, nor things present, nor things to come, nor height, nor depth, nor any other creature shall be able to separate us from the love of God which is in Christ Jesus our Lord.' Here are the benefits that God can give. That is why you 'render unto God the things that are God's'. Not only because he is God; that must come first, but all the benefits and the blessings...

See the streams of living waters,
Flowing from eternal love,
Well supply thy sons and daughters
And all fear of want remove.
Fading is the worldling's pleasure,
All his boasted pomp and show.
Solid joys and lasting treasures,
None but Zion's children know.

That is what it gives you in life, and it tells you that beyond death you are going to a glory everlasting. You are going to reign with Christ. You are going to dwell in him and bask in the sunshine of his glorious countenance, and you will be praising him and rejoicing with all others who believed in him to all eternity.

Well then, my friends, there, according to our Lord, is the message that we are to give to this troubled modern world with men's hearts failing them, with the clouds gathering and with the things by which men have lived rapidly disappearing. We must open their eyes. We must say, 'Render unto Cæsar the things that are Cæsar's *and* unto God the things that are God's.' You will begin to enjoy blessings totally beyond human imagination, which God alone can give. You will be able to smile in the face of death and even at times long to enter into that glory and to be with Christ, 'which is far better'. You and I alone can give our needy fellow men and women this message. Many can talk about politics, culture and art, and all the rest of it, but our business is to add this blessed 'and', and tell them that they are human and God's image is upon them. We must declare that they are not economic units, but are responsible beings before God, who will have to render an account unto him, and if they but realized the truth of his great gift in Jesus Christ they will not only have nothing to fear, but they will be more than conquerors, in life and in death and through all eternity.

May God give us grace to realize our commission and may he enable us to know that without the unction, the authority and the power that the Holy Spirit can give, even this message can be a dead letter. If I were to give you one word before I leave you it would be this: the supreme duty of every Christian at this hour is to pray for a mighty outpouring of the Spirit of God. Here is the message, but even the message is not enough alone. It must be in demonstration of the Spirit and of power. We must be able to say that our gospel comes to people not in word only; it must come in word, but not in word only, but in power and in the Holy Ghost and with much assurance. Pray without ceasing that in this dark hour God will revive his work again and fill us, his people, and especially preachers, with the power of the Holy Ghost. We need to be baptized again with the Holy Ghost and with power that we might proclaim these unsearchable riches of Christ. May he do so.

Let us pray.

O Lord, we come before thee, conscious of our unworthiness, conscious of the imperfection of our service, conscious of our guilt in thy holy sight. O God, awaken us, open our eyes to the battle, help us to see things as they are. Teach us to think, O Lord. Deliver us from false traditions, deliver us from sentimentality. Enable us to see the issues clearly and plainly. So reveal thyself and thy blessed truth to us that, rather than equivocate concerning it or in any way compromise it, we would sooner die. O Lord, give us this blessed power we have already prayed for, the power of thy blessed Spirit, that we may proclaim to the whole world the saving riches of thy grace. O hear us, and follow us to our homes and churches. Help us to help others to see these issues and to pray for such power upon thy Word that others will see and join us in its proclamation. Bless thy servants in this British Evangelical Council here in London and throughout the country, and use it to thy glory and to thy praise. We ask it in the name of thy dear Son, our Lord and Saviour Jesus Christ. Amen.

The British Evangelical Council enables eleven church groups from England, Scotland, Ireland and Wales to express their evangelical church unity by co-operative activities, some national, some regional and local. It comprises altogether 1,200 congregations, including those from Baptist, Congregational, Independent, Presbyterian and Pentecostal positions. All of these are, by conviction, unable to belong to church bodies where false ways of salvation are tolerated. They are convinced, however, of the importance of that evangelical ecumenism which has a genuine gospel basis.

For more information readers are invited to enquire from:

British Evangelical Council
113 Victoria Street
St Albans
AL1 3TJ
(Tel. 0727 55655)